David Helm

Daniel

Staying Strong in a
Hostile World

GOOD BOOK
GUIDE

🔽 7-Session Bible Study

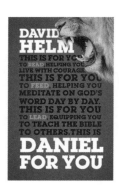

Daniel For You

These studies are adapted from *Daniel For You*. If you are reading *Daniel For You* alongside this Good Book Guide, here is how the studies in this booklet link to the chapters of *Daniel For You*:

Study 1 > Ch 1-4   Study 5 > Ch 15-17
Study 2 > Ch 5-6   Study 6 > Ch 18-21
Study 3 > Ch 7-10   Study 7 > Ch 22-26
Study 4 > Ch 11-14

Find out more about *Daniel For You* at:
www.thegoodbook.com/for-you

Daniel: Staying Strong in a Hostile World
A Good Book Guide
© David Helm/The Good Book Company 2015.
This edition printed 2025.

Published by The Good Book Company

thegoodbook.com | thegoodbook.co.uk
thegoodbook.com.au | thegoodbook.co.nz | thegoodbook.co.in

Unless indicated, all Scripture references are taken from the Holy Bible, New International Version. Copyright © 2011 Biblica. Used by permission.

David Helm has asserted his right under the Copyright, Designs and Patents Act 1988 to be identified as author of this work.

All rights reserved. Except as may be permitted by the Copyright Act, no part of this publication may be reproduced in any form or by any means without prior permission from the publisher.

A CIP catalogue record for this book is available from the British Library.

Design by André Parker and Drew McCall

ISBN: 9781802541618 | JOB-008043 | Printed in India

Contents

 # Introduction

One of the Bible writers described God's word as "a lamp for my feet, a light on my path" (Psalm 119:105, NIV). God gave us the Bible to tell us about who he is and what he wants for us. He speaks through it by his Spirit and lights our way through life.

That means that we need to look carefully at the Bible and uncover its meaning—but we also need to apply what we've discovered to our lives.

Good Book Guides are designed to help you do just that. The sessions in this book are interactive and easy to lead. They're perfect for use in groups or for personal study.

Let's take a look at what is included in each session.

Talkabout: Every session starts with an ice-breaker question, designed to get people talking around a subject that links to the Bible study.

Investigate: These questions help you explore what the passage is about.

Apply: These questions are designed to get you thinking practically: what does this Bible teaching mean for you and your church?

Explore More: These optional sections help you to go deeper or to explore another part of the Bible which connects with the main passage.

Getting Personal: These sections are a chance for personal reflection. Some groups may feel comfortable discussing these, but you may prefer to look at them quietly as individuals instead—or leave them out.

Pray: Here, you're invited to pray in the light of the truths and challenges you've seen in the study.

Each session is also designed to be easily split into two! Watch out for the **Apply** section that comes halfway through, and stop there if you haven't got time to do the whole thing in one go.

In the back of the book, you'll find a **Leader's Guide**, which provides helpful notes on every question, along with everything else that group leaders need in order to facilitate a great session and help the group uncover the riches of God's light-giving word.

Why Study Daniel?

How can we remain faithful to our God in a world that rejects him?

Is it even worth standing firm and obeying him, when his kingdom often seems so very far away?

How can we live courageously and confidently in nations that do not seek to live under God's rule?

And is it possible to be a blessing to our nations, and show the power and goodness of our God, even in a time such as ours?

Those are pressing questions for those of us who live in contexts where to be a Christian is no longer the norm (if it ever was), and is increasingly to be misunderstood, maligned, and even mistreated. And since this is the context in which Daniel found himself, the book that bears his name is one that will reassure, challenge, and thrill us as we read it today.

In chapters 1 – 6, we will see Daniel and his three friends seeking to remain faithful to God while making a home in Babylon—in the world. In chapters 7 – 12, we will find Daniel, through a series of visions, discovering how God would bring his people home from Babylon—and learning that the end of exile would not be the moment of fulfillment of God's promises of a King and a kingdom for his people.

For Daniel, that moment remained in the future, and that king a figure in the distant shadows. For us today, we can look back to the life, death, and resurrection of Jesus, and forward to his return, as the glorious moments when all this was and will be fulfilled. In many ways, we can see more clearly even than this faithful prophet of God—and yet, as these seven studies will show, how Daniel lived and what Daniel saw has so much to teach us. This book will show us what we can expect from this life, and how we can and must remain faithful and courageous in our world.

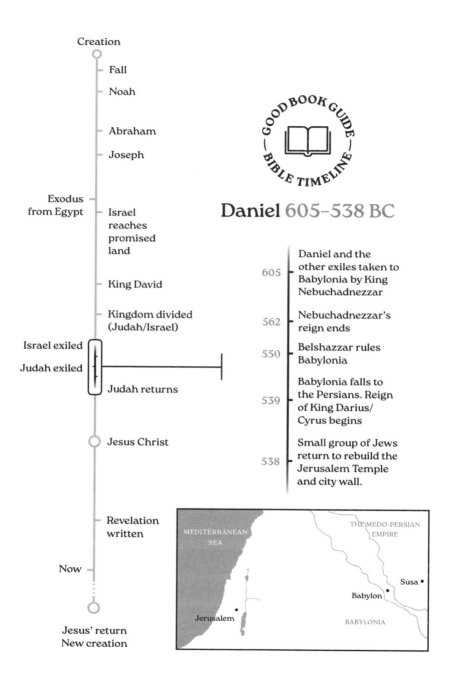

Creation

Fall

Noah

Abraham

Joseph

Exodus from Egypt

Israel reaches promised land

King David

Kingdom divided (Judah/Israel)

Israel exiled

Judah exiled

Judah returns

Jesus Christ

Revelation written

Now

Jesus' return
New creation

GOOD BOOK GUIDE
BIBLE TIMELINE

Daniel 605–538 BC

605	Daniel and the other exiles taken to Babylonia by King Nebuchadnezzar
562	Nebuchadnezzar's reign ends
550	Belshazzar rules Babylonia
539	Babylonia falls to the Persians. Reign of King Darius/Cyrus begins
538	Small group of Jews return to rebuild the Jerusalem Temple and city wall.

MEDITERRANEAN SEA

THE MEDO-PERSIAN EMPIRE

Susa

Babylon

Jerusalem

BABYLONIA

1

Babylon: Surviving and Thriving

Daniel 1 – 2

Talkabout

1. When do you find it easiest to excuse doing something you know is wrong?

Investigate

📖 **Read Daniel 1:1-7**

DICTIONARY

Judah (v 1): God's people had divided into two kingdoms: Israel and Judah.

Articles (v 2): precious objects used to worship God in the temple in Jerusalem.

---

2. When King Nebuchadnezzar takes the city of Jerusalem, what does he take into exile in Babylon (v 2-4)?

• Read Genesis 12:1-3; 2 Samuel 7:12. Why is what has happened in Jerusalem so serious?

In Daniel 1:6-7, we meet the leading characters of the first half of the book: Daniel and his three friends—four youths who were part of the deportation. They were stripped of their Jewish names and given Babylonian ones. How will they fare in Babylon? What will become of them, so far from Jerusalem? Will there be a future for God's people, as God's people?

📖 **Read Daniel 1:8-21**

DICTIONARY

Defile (v 8): make unclean or unacceptable in God's sight.

---

3. What does Daniel (and his friends) resolve not to do (v 8)?

• Why does this cause a problem, and what solution does Daniel propose (v 9-14)?

Why do the four refuse the food? Three possibilities are…
• the kind of food: it may have contradicted the dietary requirements in Leviticus 11.
• the use of the food: it may have been food taken from sacrifices to pagan gods.
• whose food it was: sharing a meal meant unity in fellowship—here, with a pagan king.

Whichever it was, it is clear that their consciences simply would not allow them to accept this food and wine.

Explore More | OPTIONAL

What makes someone into the kind of worshiper of God who will have this kind of resolve?

📖 Read 2 Kings 22 – 23

- What did King Josiah do?
- This all happened while Daniel and his friends were young and (as nobles' children) very possibly being reared in the royal palace. What does this suggest about the influence of childhood on our adulthood? How does this encourage and challenge parents? What about the wider church family?

4. How does this episode conclude (v 15-20)?

5. Reread verses 2, 9, and 17. In each verse, God "gives" someone something. For each, pick out what he gave and to whom.

Apply

6. How does knowing that God gives, on both a national level and in personal ways, change the way we view life?

- How does it encourage us to follow our consciences, even when this could be costly?

Getting Personal | OPTIONAL

Has there been a time (perhaps it is now) when your conscience has urged you to follow a potentially difficult path? Did you listen to your conscience, or bow to pressure? Next time you're in a similar situation, what truths do you need to remember that will give you the strength to follow your conscience?

Investigate

📖 **Read Daniel 2:1-13**

7. Why can the king's advisers not explain his dream to him (v 10-11)?

- Why is this serious news for Daniel and his friends (v 12-13)?

📖 **Read Daniel 2:14-23**

DICTIONARY

Mercy (v 18): here, being spared punishment (by having the dream revealed to them by God).

Deposes (v 21): removes from power.

---

8. When God reveals the content and meaning of the king's dream to Daniel, how does Daniel respond (v 20-23)?

• What truths about God are we reminded of in these verses?

📖 **Read Daniel 2:24-49**

DICTIONARY

Chaff (v 35): the inedible husks of corn, blown away by the wind when the grain was "threshed."

Incense (v 46): sweet-smelling substance.

9. What was the content of the dream (v 31-35)?

10. What is the interpretation of the dream (v 36-45)?

11. Why would the words "after you" (v 39) have been a great relief to Nebuchadnezzar?

12. What were the rise and fall of various powerful empires all heading toward (v 44-45)?

- Read Luke 20:17-19. How does Jesus link the image of Daniel 2:44-45 to himself?

Apply

Nebuchadnezzar needed to hear that the major event in history would be the coming of the stone—and we now know that the stone is Christ. He is the one who replaces all humanity's self-rule—who, in fact, smashes it.

13. How is this both exciting for us and a warning to us?

- Remember that the meaning of the dream was intended for the pagan king, not the godly servant. What does this mean for us today?

Getting Personal | OPTIONAL

Daniel is not only pointing us to Jesus; he is also an example to us. Daniel told the king that God was speaking to him, through the dream. We are to tell the world that God is speaking to it, through Jesus. Wherever God has placed you, remember this: he has a word to be made known.

What difference will it make this month if you see yourself as having been placed where you are by God to make his word known and intelligible?

Pray

Turn the words of Daniel 2:20-23 into your prayer of praise, thanking God for revealing his wisdom to the world in the person of Jesus Christ. Ask God to use you to make his word known.

Pray for the resolve to follow your conscience even when that's difficult. Pray through any particular situations you have shared together.

2

Faithful in the Fire

Daniel 3

The Story So Far...

Exiled in Babylon, Daniel and his friends remained committed to worshiping God, who gave Daniel wisdom as he announced God's coming kingdom.

Talkabout

1. What statements do people or organizations make through building impressive structures or buildings?

Investigate

At the end of Daniel 2, the king honored Daniel and, remarkably, recognized that the God of Israel was truly God (v 47). But this does not mean he has himself understood who the God of the Bible really is, or what he does.

📖 **Read Daniel 3:1-7**

DICTIONARY

Cubit (v 1): about 18 inches or 45 cm.
Satrap (v 2): an official in charge of an area of land.

Zither, lyre (v 5): stringed musical instruments.

---

2. What does Nebuchadnezzar make, and for what purpose?

3. In which verses do we see reference made to King Nebuchadnezzar and the words "set up"? What point is being made by this repetition?

📖 **Read Daniel 3:8-18**

Shadrach, Meshach, and Abednego have been enjoying favor with the king (2:49).

4. How does that now change (3:8-15)?

5. What choice do the three face?

6. What do they choose (v 16-18)?

• How are they answering the question the king asks them in verse 15?

Apply

It is all too easy to stand in judgment of Nebuchadnezzar, and identify with Daniel's three courageous friends. But if we are honest, we should all primarily identify with the king.

7. How can we (on a smaller scale) act as the king does in verses 1-7?

So how should we learn from the three friends and their faithfulness? By learning to read this story in light of the gospel.

8. Read Matthew 4:8-10. What are the similarities between Daniel 3 and this passage, and between the choice made by the three Jews and by Jesus?

Getting Personal | OPTIONAL

Shadrach, Meshach, and Abednego point us to the greater faithfulness to God that Jesus modeled for us, not only during his temptation in the wilderness but on every occasion—and against a stronger ruler by far! Jesus gave his life, every waking moment, to worshiping God and serving him alone. And that took him to a place of death that he did not shirk—to our place of death, where our death died because he took it for us.

How does Christ's perfect, permanent faithfulness encourage you to repent where needed, and motivate you to remain faithful today?

Investigate

📖 **Read Daniel 3:19-30**

Explore More | OPTIONAL

In the Bible, fire is associated with two things.

📖 **Read Genesis 19:24; Revelation 19:20**

• What is the first association?

📖 **Read Malachi 3:1-4; 1 Corinthians 3:11-15**

• What is the other?

Fire destroys; but it also tests, and reveals the true nature of something. Fire will burn us up, or it will be the occasion of our salvation.

We will look at Daniel 3:19-30 in more detail next; but when it comes to the king's fiery furnace, what kind of fire…

• did he intend it to be?
• did God use it to be?

---

9. How is the furnace described (v 19-22)? Why is this emphasized, do you think?

• So why do the three Jews end up in the state they are in by verses 26-27?

10. How does the king respond (v 28-30)?

• What has changed in his view of himself? (Compare verses 4-5.)

- How has his view of the God of Israel changed? (Compare the end of verse 15.)

Apply

11. Read 1 Peter 4:12-14. What will happen as we live as God's people in this world?

- How should we view that?

12. God brought these three believers through the fire. Read 1 Peter 1:3-9. In what sense do we know God will bring us through the "fire" of trials?

13. What difference will believing this make...
- when we face the choice between compromise and faithfulness?

- when we are in a trial because we are living faithfully?

Getting Personal | OPTIONAL

What is most difficult in your life at the moment? Are you tempted to see it as judgment? What would change if you viewed it as refinement—as proving the genuineness of your faith?

Pray

Thank Jesus for his perfect faithfulness in facing the judgment his people deserve.

Pray that you would show the same faithfulness as Shadrach, Meshach, and Abednego when you are under pressure to compromise with the world.

Ask God to use the trials in your life to refine you and prove the genuineness of your faith. Pray for those in your church family who are experiencing particularly painful trials.

3

Humbled and Restored

Daniel 4

The Story So Far...

Exiled in Babylon, Daniel and his friends remained committed to worshiping God, who gave Daniel wisdom as he announced God's coming kingdom.

Nebuchadnezzar commanded worship of the image he had built; Daniel's friends refused and were thrown into the furnace—but God rescued them.

Talkabout

1. What do people take pride in?

• Can it ever be a good thing to lose what makes us proud? Why / how?

Investigate

📖 **Read Daniel 4:1-3**

Dominion (v 3): territory or kingdom;
or power to rule.

2. Who is speaking here?

- Given what we have seen of him in Daniel 1 – 3, what is striking about his words here?

3. How is the king's message…
   - something public?

   - something personal? (Note: A better translation of the end of verse 1 is "Peace be multiplied to you!")

   - centered on God and his kingdom?

These themes are the main melody of the entire book of Daniel—these distinctive notes will recur time and time again (and have already appeared) in the book. But what could cause these great truths to come from the lips of the most powerful king in the known world—and a pagan?! We are about to see…

📖 **Read Daniel 4:4-27**

DICTIONARY

Diviners (v 7): used supernatural powers to see into the future or the unknown.

Holy one (v 13): set apart and pure.
Sovereign (v 17): in total control.
Adversaries (v 19): enemies.

4. What is the content of the dream (v 9-17)?

   • How does it make the king feel (v 5)?

5. Sum up Daniel's God-given interpretation of the dream in verses 24-27.

6. How do Daniel's words to the king show us…
   • his love for the king (v 19)?

   • his honesty?

   • God's purpose in all this (v 25-26)?

Apply

7. Daniel is a believer in God, telling truth to an unbeliever. What does his example teach us about our own witness?

Getting Personal | OPTIONAL

We need to know what it is to be able to say, as Paul does in Romans 10:1, "Brothers and sisters, my heart's desire and prayer to God for the Israelites is that they may be saved."

Is your heart tender toward those who don't know God? What might a tendency to keep quiet about Christ suggest about you?

Investigate

📖 **Read Daniel 4:28-37**

DICTIONARY

Seven times (v 32): a figure of speech meaning a set amount of time that God has already decided.

Exalt (v 37): speak highly of.

"All this happened to King Nebuchadnezzar" (v 28).

8. What was the king thinking as his humiliation arrived (v 29-30)?

Verse 29 suggests that Nebuchadnezzar heeded Daniel's advice (v 27) for a year. But the true inner man re-emerges in verse 30; pride always finds its voice.

9. Whose words were more powerful and accurate: the king's or heaven's?

10. What are we being taught about human achievements and pride in such things?

11. What did Nebuchadnezzar do, and what then happened (v 34, 36)?

12. What had this powerful king now learned to do (v 34-35, 37)?

- Why was it a good thing for the king to lose everything that he had achieved and to be utterly humiliated?

Apply

13. How is Nebuchadnezzar's experience here a very dramatic picture of what happens in every conversion?

- Share some examples of God breaking someone's pride in order to bring them to worship and praise him—either from your own life or from those of others you know.

Getting Personal | OPTIONAL

Has God brought you to a place in your life that has you crawling on your knees even now? If so, why not see Nebuchadnezzar as your example? Why not pray something like this? "Dear God, my pride has nearly ruined me. Your power has nearly overwhelmed me, and I have been brought low. Please change me. Put new clothes upon me. Give to me the robes of Christ's righteousness, that I may rise from this desperate and deranged state, and give you the praise that is due to you from me."

Explore More | OPTIONAL

📖 **Read Luke 22:31-34, 54-62**

- How do we see God breaking another man's pride in his own abilities so that he might come to truly love and follow the Lord Jesus?
- How does this both humble and comfort us?

Pray

Look back at your answer to question 12. Give God praise and glory for his work in your own life and the lives of those people you talked about. Use the words of Daniel 4:3, 34-35 and 37 to echo King Nebuchadnezzar's exuberant praise.

Confess times when you take pride in your own position and achievements. Ask God to make you humble before him.

Pray that you would share Daniel's tender heart toward those who do not know God. Perhaps pray specifically for some individuals you find it especially difficult to be tenderhearted toward.

4

Who Rules?
Kings vs. God

Daniel 5 - 6

The Story So Far...

Exiled in Babylon, Daniel and his friends remained committed to worshiping God, who gave Daniel wisdom as he announced God's coming kingdom.

Nebuchadnezzar commanded worship of the image he had built; Daniel's friends refused and were thrown into the furnace—but God rescued them.

God brought proud King Nebuchadnezzar low in order to bring him into his eternal kingdom. God's word is a public proclamation offering peace.

Talkabout

1. How can you tell that someone trusts in God?

Investigate

📖 **Read Daniel 5:1-31**

DICTIONARY

Concubines (v 3): a slave used as a live-in mistress.

Medes and Persians (v 28): other nations; Babylon's enemies.

---

2. Write down in three or four sentences a summary of the events of the chapter, and what you think the meaning of it is for us.

3. What is the king trying to prove by his actions in verses 2-4, do you think?

4. What should Belshazzar have known to do, and why (v 22)?

- How does God respond, both in what he promises and in what happens (v 28, 30)?

5. Daniel knew the Lord's verdict when he refused the king's offer (v 16-17). How would knowing how things would play out affect his perspective on what the king was offering?

Apply

In the previous study, we saw a king humbled in order for him to acknowledge God and be raised up. Here, we see a king who refuses to acknowledge God and mocks him—and is deposed and killed.

6. How does this warn us about the pride in our own hearts?

- How does it teach us to view this world?

Investigate

📖 **Read Daniel 6:1-28**

DICTIONARY

Reverence (v 26): show great respect to.

7. Write down in three or four sentences a summary of the events of the chapter, and what you think the meaning of it is for us.

8. What is striking about the only way Daniel's enemies can find a reason to accuse him (v 4-5)?

• Why were they so determined to bring him down, do you think?

Getting Personal | OPTIONAL

The Persian officials were "unable" to "find grounds for charges against Daniel in his conduct of government affairs" (v 4). His books were in order. His numbers all added up. No bribes had been taken and witnesses to the contrary could not be found.

The only accusation that stuck against Daniel was that he would not stop worshiping his God. Would that be true of you in your working life too? Why / why not?

---

9. How do verses 10-15 contrast the resolute courage of Daniel and the weakness of the king?

10. In what sense is Daniel's God, as well as Daniel himself, on trial (v 16)?

11. So what does Daniel's rescue reveal about…
   • God (v 20-22, 26-27)?

- Daniel (v 22-23)?

Explore More | OPTIONAL

- Imagine you were one of the 122 who had successfully accused Daniel. Trace how well or badly things are going for you through the chapter. Then put yourself in Daniel's position and do the same thing.
- How does this teach us, as God's people, to view life, opposition, and times when those who oppose God's people thrive?

12. What similarities do you see between Daniel in chapter 6 and Jesus in the Gospels?

Apply

13. What flaws do we see in those around Daniel in these two episodes?

- How does Daniel show us what it means to believe in the sovereign, saving God of the Bible?

- Discuss what these flaws, and this faithfulness, would look like in your particular culture and settings today.

Getting Personal | OPTIONAL

Daniel 6:28 is a summary which brings the first half of the book to a close: "So Daniel prospered during the reign of Darius and the reign of Cyrus the Persian." For over 70 years, Daniel "prospered." He learned how to remain faithful and fruitful, and how to be at home in Babylon.

Look back on the last four studies and reflect: how have you been helped to live both faithfully and fruitfully in the world?

Pray

Thank the Lord that he is "the living God," who rescues and saves (v 26-27). Thank God that Jesus faced a death that he didn't deserve, and was raised from the tomb to assure us of the power of his saving death.

Look back at your answer to question 12 and...

- *confess those times when you have displayed these flaws.*
- *ask God to help you live faithfully in the ways you discussed.*

5

One Like a Son of Man

Daniel 7

The Story So Far...

Nebuchadnezzar commanded worship of the image he had built; Daniel's friends refused and were thrown into the furnace—but God rescued them.

God brought proud King Nebuchadnezzar low in order to bring him into his eternal kingdom. God's word is a public proclamation offering peace.

Daniel refused to stop praying to God, and was thrown in the lions' den. But God delivered him, proving himself to be the God who is real, and who can rescue.

Talkabout

1. What do you think your life as a Christian will be like between now and the day you die or when Jesus returns? Why do you think this?

Investigate

In Daniel 7 (and for the rest of the book) the genre shifts from narrative to apocalyptic. Apocalyptic literature is often viewed as too difficult to understand—many give up reading Daniel at the end of chapter 6.

But it is helpful to think about apocalyptic literature as painting a picture, or providing a movie. Its purpose is to reveal (the word *apokalypsis* means "revelation")—to pull back the curtain and show us an unseen, transcendent world. God wrote Daniel 7 – 12 wanting us to understand and be shaped by what it says—we should read it with expectation and confidence.

📖 Read Daniel 7:1-8

Previously, dreams came to the king, and we have seen that this was because God intended them as a message for the world.

2. This time the dream comes to Daniel, and not to the king (v 1). Why is that significant?

Apocalyptic literature is full of symbols—things that are to be taken figuratively. And the symbol can stand *both* for a particular event, person, or place *and* for a more general principle that holds true for more than one event, person, or place.

3. What does Daniel see in this dream (v 2-8)?

• Read verse 17. What do these beasts represent?

There are two ways to understand the specific kingdoms they point to:

First beast = Babylonian	First beast = Babylonian
Second = Medo-Persian	Second = Mede
Third = Greek	Third = Persian
Fourth = Roman	Fourth = Greek

4. Read Revelation 13:1-3. What do you notice about this symbolic description of Rome? What does this tell you about what the symbols in Daniel 7 stand for more generally?

📖 Read Daniel 7:9-14

DICTIONARY

Ancient of Days (v 9): a name for God which reflects his ageless nature.

5. After the rise of the fourth beast, what happens next (v 9-10)?

• What does the Ancient of Days do (v 11-12)?

6. Who does Daniel see next (v 13-14)? Where is this person, and what is he given?

• Read Mark 14:53, 60-64. Who is the "one like a son of man" whom Daniel saw?

- Read Philippians 2:8-11. When did he approach the Ancient of Days to receive universal power and authority?

Getting Personal | OPTIONAL

You know the Son of Man is your Savior, reigning in heaven right now. In what area of your life do you most need to remember this truth? How will that change your perspective, feelings, and/or actions?

Explore More | OPTIONAL

📖 **Read Psalm 2**

- How does this psalm also refer to the themes that Daniel sees in his vision?

Apply

7. Every worldly power (the "beasts") looked extremely strong and irresistible to Daniel—and they still do to us today. What does Daniel 7:9-10 remind us of?

- How should this affect how we respond to news about oppressive political systems, and to the ungodly demands of our own rulers?

Investigate

📖 **Read Daniel 7:15-28**

Holy people (v 18): those who follow God.

Subdue (v 24): bring under control.

Time, times and half a time (v 25): see session 7. A length of time that God has already decided.

Daniel is "troubled" and asks for "the meaning of all this" (v 15-16).

8. How would verses 17-18 have encouraged him?

Next, he asks for further clarification on the "meaning of the fourth beast" (v 19), and is given an "explanation" (v 23).

9. How does that explanation leave him feeling (v 28)?

• Why would verses 23-25 have made him feel like that?

Daniel knew (from Jeremiah 29:10-14—see Daniel 9:2) that the exile in Babylon would last 70 years. Before receiving this vision, he may well have thought that once the 70 years of exile were over, things would be bright for the family of God.

10. How is this dream in Daniel 7 (and particularly this last explanation) reshaping his expectations?

Apply

11. How should Daniel's dream reshape our expectations of...
    • our future between today and the day Jesus returns?

    • our future beyond the day Jesus returns?

12. What difference will having a Daniel-7 perspective of our present and our future make, day by day?

13. What will go wrong if we forget...
    • what life is like for God's people as they travel through life toward home in God's kingdom?

    • what life is like for God's people once they reach their home in God's kingdom?

Getting Personal | OPTIONAL

How are you currently experiencing the difficulties of life as a member of God's people on their way home? One day "the court will sit" (v 26). How might you help yourself to remember this truth in the midst of difficulties?

Pray

Thank God that one day his kingdom will prevail, "the court will sit," and Christ will judge those who oppose him. Ask him to give you a "Daniel-7 perspective" on your present and your future.

Pray for Christians in other parts of the world who are oppressed and persecuted by unjust governments. Pray that the knowledge of God's certain victory would help them to persevere.

6

Daniel's Prayer

Daniel 8 - 9

The Story So Far...

God brought proud King Nebuchadnezzar low in order to bring him into his eternal kingdom. God's word is a public proclamation offering peace.

Daniel refused to stop praying to God, and was thrown in the lions' den. But God delivered him, proving himself to be the God who is real, and who can rescue.

God's kingdom, ruled by the Son of Man, Jesus, will prevail and defeat ungodly earthly kingdoms; but life will be hard for his people until that day comes.

Talkabout

1. Why do we pray? What stops us from praying?

Investigate

📖 **Read Daniel 8:1-27**

DICTIONARY

Citadel of Susa (v 2): a fortress 200 miles away from Babylon.
Beautiful Land (v 9): Israel.

Host (v 10): stars.
Daily sacrifice (v 11): act of worship to God in the Jerusalem Temple.

Sanctuary (v 11): the most holy part of the temple.
Reconsecrated (v 14): made fit for worship again.

Prostrate (v 17): lying flat on the ground, face down.
Wrath (v 19): deserved anger.

2. Describe the vision Daniel sees in verses 2-12. (You may like to draw it.)

3. What will the "horn" do in the "Beautiful Land" (v 11-12, 23-25)?

• How will things end up (v 14, 25)?

4. Read John 2:19-22; Hebrews 10:11-14. In what sense was Jesus the final fulfillment of Daniel 8:14?

Apply

5. How does this vision once again underline the way God's people need to look at their present and their future?

Investigate

📖 **Read Daniel 9:1-19**

Jeremiah the prophet (v 2): Jeremiah delivered a message from God that Judah would be taken into exile by the Babylonians.
Desolation (v 2): time of destruction.

Covenant (v 4): legal agreement.
Righteous (v 7): in the right.
Transgressed (v 11): broken.
Iniquities (v 16): wrong behavior.

Throughout the book, Daniel has been characterized as a man of prayer (2:17-18, 19-23; 6:10). Here, we have the most detailed of his prayers in the book that bears his name.

6. What prompted Daniel's prayer (9:2-3)?

• Read Jeremiah 29:10-14. Why is it strange that Daniel responds in "sackcloth and ashes"—clothes that signify an attitude of mourning (Daniel 9:3)?

7. How does Daniel 9:4-16 show why Daniel dressed like this?

8. But Daniel himself was "innocent in [God's] sight" (6:22). What does his identification with all God's people, and his confession as a member of that people, teach us about our prayers?

Getting Personal | OPTIONAL

For Daniel, confession runs along two lines. Not only is it saying something about the wrongs we have committed against God—our sin—but it is saying something about the merciful character of God—his righteousness.

Do your private prayer times include much confession? Do you see confession as merely one-dimensional (confessing to God the things you've done wrong)? How can you get into the habit of meditating on God's righteousness as you confess your sins?

9. On what basis does Daniel dare to plead to God to keep his promises (9:17-19)?

10. We have seen the innocent Daniel praying on behalf of God's people. Read Romans 8:34; 1 John 2:1. How is he picturing what Jesus is doing for us right now?

Explore More | OPTIONAL

📖 Read Ezra 1:2-4, 6-7

These events took place shortly after Daniel's prayer in Daniel 9.

- How did God both keep his promise of Jeremiah 29 and answer Daniel's prayer?

📖 Read Daniel 9:20-27

DICTIONARY

Holy hill (v 20): Jerusalem.
Atone (v 24): make up for.
Anoint (v 24): pour oil over something to show it's been set

apart for a special role.
Abomination (v 27): a thing which causes disgust.

11. Who appears, when, and why (v 20-23)?

Daniel had asked God to make an end to the 70 years of exile as he had promised through Jeremiah. Now Daniel discovers it will take another "seventy sevens" before a complete deliverance will come! Israel's return to the land will not be a complete return from "exile."

12. But, when the time finally comes, what will happen (v 24)?

- How is this pointing us toward Jesus—both his death and resurrection, and his return—as the final fulfillment?

Explore More | OPTIONAL

📖 **Reread Daniel 9:25-27**

- Can you trace out four stages that will take place?

These verses are not straightforward! Apocalyptic literature is often fulfilled in more than one person, or event, or time. So the "Anointed One" could refer to the Persian ruler Cyrus, who allowed the Jews back to Jerusalem (see Isaiah 45:1); or Joshua, high priest at the time of the temple's rebuilding (Haggai 1:1); or Zerubbabel, who led the first group who returned to construct the temple.

The anointed one who was cut off could be Onias III (the Jewish high priest murdered around 175 BC), or Jesus Christ.

And the second half of verse 26 likely has AD 70 and the final destruction of the temple in view. The important thing to note is that all this happens in history—God was telling Daniel he would be at work throughout the "seventy sevens" to bring about the salvation of his people.

Apply

13. How have these chapters encouraged you about why God's people pray? Look back at your answer to question 1. Which of the reasons why we find prayer hard can Daniel 8 – 9 help us with?

Getting Personal | OPTIONAL

Verse 23 says the speedy response to Daniel's prayer came for he was "greatly loved" (ESV). Centuries later, Jesus encouraged his followers in the same way: "Which of you fathers, if your son asks for a fish, will give him a snake instead? Or if he asks for an egg, will give him a scorpion? If you then, though you are evil, know how to give good gifts to your children, how much more will your Father in heaven give the Holy Spirit to those who ask him!" (Luke 11:11-13).

In which area of your prayer life do you most need to hear this encouragement and comfort? What difference would it make to your commitment to prayer if you remembered this?

Pray

By now you should be eager to pray! Shape your prayers around the pattern we see in Daniel 9:

- *A reflection on God's promises in his word, and his righteous, powerful, and merciful character.*
- *Humble confession as you identify with the failings of your whole church.*
- *Petition based on God's mercy, and confidence in his gracious promises, rather than any sense of entitlement.*

Be encouraged, knowing that as you pray, Christ is also praying on your behalf. And remember that God delights to answer the prayers of his people: "For you are greatly loved" (Daniel 9:23, ESV).

7

The Final Vision

Daniel 10 - 12

The Story So Far...

Daniel refused to stop praying to God, and was thrown in the lions' den. But God delivered him, proving himself to be the God who is real, and who can rescue.

God's kingdom, ruled by the Son of Man, Jesus, will prevail and defeat ungodly earthly kingdoms; but life will be hard for his people until that day comes.

Daniel prayed in response to God's word and God's character, confessing on behalf of the Jews and asking God mercifully to return them from exile.

Talkabout

1. What events or possibilities in your future most affect your actions and feelings in the present?

Investigate

📖 **Read Daniel 10:1 – 11:1**

-- DICTIONARY

Topaz (v 6): precious stone.
Burnished (v 6): polished.
Multitude (v 6): crowd of many people.

Prince (v 13): powerful spiritual being.

2. Why is Daniel the only person to see the vision (v 4-9)?

• How does he feel about seeing the "man dressed in linen" (v 8, 11, 16-17)?

3. What are we seeing about the costs of being a prophet? How different is this from what you tend to think being a prophet would have been like?

Getting Personal | OPTIONAL

Hearing the word of God and passing it on is sometimes dangerous and always difficult. Gospel proclamation is costly.

Who do you know who is engaged in gospel ministry whom you could encourage more, or pray for more?

Explore More | OPTIONAL

📖 **Reread Daniel 10:12-14; 10:20 – 11:1**

• Why did the angel not join Daniel earlier?

These verses pull back the veil on the unseen universe—there is not merely an angelic host who do the bidding of God, but there are fallen ones, who work to oppose his will. And it appears that God has fixed the borders of nations according to assignments given to angels. (See Deuteronomy 32:8-9, where "sons of Israel" or "sons of God" (ESV) may refer to angels.)

- How does this glimpse of the unseen universe humble us as 21st-century humans?

📖 Read Daniel 11:1-35

DICTIONARY

Insolence (v 18): rudeness and disrespect.
Contemptible (v 21): completely worthless; disgusting.

Desecrate (v 31): make unfit for worship.

Again, Daniel is told about the rise and fall of kingdoms; again, in verses 21-35, the rule of Antiochus Epiphanes is most in view (though remember that symbols stand for general principles as well as specific people).

4. What effect will his reign have on God's people (v 28, 30-32)?

- What mistakes will God's people make, or be tempted to make (v 14, 30, 32)?

- What will "the wise" do (v 32-35)?

Apply

We should not read apocalyptic literature for its "otherness" so much as for its "oughtness." We need to finish reading it by asking ourselves: *now what ought I to do?*

5. What would it look like for us as God's people to make the mistakes of verses 14, 30, and 32?

- How ought we to apply verses 32-35 to ourselves? (Read Mark 13:5-13, 32-37 for Jesus' help in answering this!)

Investigate

📖 Read Daniel 12:1-13

6. What will happen when deliverance finally arrives (v 2-3)?

7. What must Daniel do, and until when (v 4)?

- Read 1 Peter 1:10-12. In what sense do we live in "the time of the end"? (See the words of the angel to Daniel in 12:4.)

8. What question is asked in verse 6?

- What answer is given, and how does Daniel feel about that answer (v 7-8)?

In Revelation 12:14, the phrase "time, times and half a time" is used to refer to the season of persecution which the church endures from Satan, between the death and resurrection of Christ and his final return. So it may well be that the angel is telling Daniel that the final fulfillment—including the resurrection of God's people from the dead—will come only when Christ returns.

9. How should Daniel (and we) respond to this glimpse of the future (v 12-13)?

Remember that Daniel received these visions while he lived in Babylon— while he was explaining the writing on the wall to King Belshazzar and refusing to cease praying under the reign of King Darius.

10. How would the truths about God, the world, and the future that were revealed in these visions have enabled him to live as he did in Babylon, do you think?

Apply

11. How does verse 13 both encourage and challenge you as a believer today?

12. What difference has the book of Daniel made to...
    • your view of God?

    • your understanding of what it will mean for you to worship him?

    • your obedience in difficult circumstances?

Getting Personal | OPTIONAL

Look at your answer to question 12. Are there any practical steps you need to take in response to what you've learned from the book of Daniel?

Pray

Spend time thanking God for the promise of eternal life, and that one day his people "will be purified, made spotless and refined" (Daniel 12:10).

Pray for those individuals involved in costly gospel ministry whom you thought of in response to the Getting Personal section on page 44.

Ask God to help each member of your group to labor on faithfully, in Christ, toward your rest.

Daniel

*Staying Strong in a
Hostile World*

Leader's Guide: Introduction

This Leader's Guide includes guidance for every question. It will provide background information and help you if you get stuck. For each session, you'll also find the following:

The Big Idea: The main point of the session, in brief. This is what you should be aiming to have fixed in people's minds by the end of the session!

Summary: An overview of the passage you're reading together.

Optional Extra: Usually this is an introductory activity that ties in with the main theme of the Bible study and is designed to break the ice at the beginning of a session. Or it may be a "homework project" that people can tackle during the week.

Occasionally the Leader's Guide includes an extra follow-up question, printed in *italics*. This doesn't appear in the main study guide but could be a useful add-on to help your group get to the answer or go deeper.

Here are a few key principles to bear in mind as you prepare to lead:

- Don't just read out the answers from the Leader's Guide. Ideally, you want the group to discover these answers from the Bible for themselves.

- Keep drawing people back to the passage you're studying. People may come up with answers based on their experiences or on teaching they've heard in the past, but the point of this study is to listen to God's word itself—so keep directing your group to look at the text.

- Make sure everyone finishes the session knowing how the passage is relevant for them. We do Bible study so that our lives can be changed by what we hear from God's word. So, **Apply** questions aren't just an add-on—they're a vital part of the session.

Finally, remember that your group is unique! You should feel free to use this Good Book Guide in a way that works for them. If they're a quiet bunch, you might want to spend longer on the **Talkabout** question. If they love to get creative, try using mind-mapping or doodling to kick-start some of your discussions. If your time is limited, you can choose to skip **Explore More** or split the whole session into two. Adapt the material in whatever way you think will help your group get the most out of God's word.

1

Babylon: Surviving and Thriving

Daniel 1 - 2

The Big Idea

In the middle of a crisis, Daniel remains committed to worshiping God, and God gives him favor and understanding, making him a blessing to those around him in Babylon, as God announces his coming kingdom to the world.

Summary

The book of Daniel opens with a crisis (1:1-7). Nebuchadnezzar, the ruler of the powerful empire centered on Babylon, had besieged Jerusalem, the capital of Judah, the land God had promised his people and protected them in. When he took the city, he defeated Judah's king, and deported to Babylon the brightest and the best of Judah's people, and the items used in temple worship. Among these people were the main characters of the first half of the book: Daniel and his friends—Shadrach, Meshach, and Abednego.

The rest of this study focuses on two episodes in the life of these four in the king's court in Babylon. First, Daniel and his friends refuse to eat the king's food and drink his wine—but they nevertheless look healthier than their contemporaries, grow in understanding, and are taken into the king's service (1:8-21). We are being taught to live according to our consciences, even when that is risky. And we see

that at every point, it is God who is in charge, giving Nebuchadnezzar victory in Jerusalem, giving the four wisdom, giving Daniel favor. We obey God because we know he is at work.

Second, God gives Daniel the ability to interpret a dream the king has (2:1-49). Daniel is the man of wisdom, through whom heaven makes knowledge available. And the dream both assures the king that his kingdom will last beyond his own lifetime, and announces the coming of a "rock" that will smash all other kingdoms and fill the earth—the kingdom of God. In this study, we see that the Lord Jesus identified himself with this "rock," and his death and resurrection as the means of its coming. In giving the dream to the pagan king, not to one of his own people, God is giving this message to the world, not merely to "the church"; and it is the same in our day.

Optional Extra

Before you begin, ask your group to think of everything they know about the book of Daniel. This will help you see how familiar they are with the book as a whole, rather than simply the famous parts (the fiery furnace, the lions' den, the Son of Man vision). Ask them to suggest what they think the book of Daniel is all about—you could then return to this at the end of session 7 to summarize how group members have moved forward in their understanding and application of the book.

Guidance for Questions

1. **When do you find it easiest to excuse doing something you know is wrong?**

Answers will of course vary, but some common ones are…
- when we are alone
- when we are away from home
- when we are surrounded by others who see no problem with that conduct
- when we feel we will lose out if we don't do it, or will gain greatly from doing it.

You might like to point out after question 3 or 6 that these were the circumstances in which Daniel and his friends found themselves in Daniel 1:8-21.

2. **When King Nebuchadnezzar takes the city of Jerusalem, what does he take into exile in Babylon (v 2-4)?**
- v 2: Jehoiakim, the king of Judah i.e. God's people (see 2 Chronicles 36:5-6).
- v 2: "Some of the articles from the temple of God" in Jerusalem— items used in temple worship.
- v 3-4: The best and the brightest young people in Judah.

The king is defeated, and the people are deported.

- **Read Genesis 12:1-3; 2 Samuel 7:12. Why is what has happened in Jerusalem so serious?**

Because God has promised to bless Abraham's descendants (i.e. Israel, or Judah); and, through them, people from all over the earth, and to give them a land to dwell in (Genesis 12:1-3); and to do so by giving his people a king who will be descended from King David, and rule for ever (2 Samuel 7:12-13). If the Davidic dynasty has ended, and the people are no longer in their land, then it would appear to mark the end, not only of a king over Judah and the continuance of God's people, but also of the promises of God.

3. **What does Daniel (and his friends) resolve not to do (v 8)?**

Become defiled by eating the king's food and drinking his wine. Notice the word "defiled" is repeated for emphasis.

- **Why does this cause a problem, and what solution does Daniel propose (v 9-14)?**

The king's chief official is worried he will be in life-threatening trouble with the king if they end up "looking worse than the other young men" (v 10). So Daniel suggests a ten-day experiment in which the four will eat only vegetables and drink only water (v 11-12), and then their appearances will be compared to others' (v 13).

Explore More

- o **Read 2 Kings 22 – 23. What did King Josiah do?**
  - He repaired the temple (22:3-5).
  - He recovered the Book of the Law (v 8-11).
  - He called for repentance (23:13, 18-19).
  - He led reforms (v 4-25).
  - He returned God's word to the center of Israel's life (v 1-3).
  - He deposed ungodly priests (v 5).
  - He restored the celebration of Passover (v 21-23).

- o **This all happened while Daniel and his friends were young and (as nobles' children) very possibly being reared in the royal palace. What does this suggest about the influence of childhood on our adulthood? How does this encourage and challenge parents? What about the wider church family?**

  People of resolve are fashioned; they are made. So raising children matters; it is a time when godly character and resolve are formed. Much of who we are as adults is shaped by how we are raised as children. We need to ask ourselves: what kind of young people are we raising in our church? Raising children for God is one of the most important businesses done on earth—and all Christians, whether parents or not, are involved in this business, because we are all part of a church family. We need to be committed to growing "Daniels." Spend time discussing how your church, and
  any individual families represented in your group, are seeking to do this, and praying for this. Make sure your interaction is encouraging, rather than guilt-inducing.

---

4. **How does this episode conclude (v 15-20)?**
   - v 15: At the end of the experiment, Daniel and his friends looked better, not worse, than their contemporaries.
   - v 17: God gave them knowledge and understanding in their studies.
   - v 19-20: They were ten times better than the other "wise men" working for the king, and so were taken into his service.

5. **Reread verses 2, 9, and 17. In each verse, God "gives" someone something. For each, pick out what he gave and to whom.**
   - v 2: God delivered (literally "gave") the king of Judah into the king of Babylon's hands.
   - v 9: God caused the official to be generous to Daniel. He literally "gave" Daniel favor in this man's eyes.
   - v 17: God gave Daniel and his three friends wisdom and understanding.

- o **OPTIONAL: What are we meant to understand by these subtle lines about God "giving"?**
  God is in charge. Ultimately it is him moving the wheel of history to accomplish his ends; he is in control even over crises, and even over the

most powerful people in the world. And God is in charge of individuals, and cares for his people, giving favor and compassion to those from whom it is needed, and giving his people the abilities they need to serve him and be useful in the world. God is at work on a grand scale and a personal level; nothing is an accident.

6. How does knowing that God gives, on both a national level and in personal ways, change the way we view life?

We will not be dismayed by, nor despair at, apparent catastrophes. God was at work in the fall of Jerusalem and the exile of its young elite; he will be at work in, and in control of, all that happens in our world.

We will make commitments, as Daniel did, to remain morally and religiously pure in a pagan world. We'll engage with the world, rather than running from it, trusting God to give us what we need (whatever that should prove to be), and to make us useful to others according to his purposes.

• How does it encourage us to follow our consciences, even when this could be costly?

Because we know there is one in charge to whom we are accountable. And because we know that we can leave the outcomes up to him, and simply get on with obeying him.

7. Why can the king's advisers not explain his dream to him (v 10-11)?

Because the king has not even told them what his dream is (v 2, 4). With no description of the dream, they cannot provide any kind of explanation; the king is asking the impossible—that they should know what only "the gods" understand (v 11).

• Why is this serious news for Daniel and his friends (v 12-13)?

Because, due to the events of 1:17-20, Daniel and his three friends are now numbered among those deemed wise—and therefore are now among those due to be executed.

8. When God reveals the content and meaning of the king's dream to Daniel, how does Daniel respond (v 20-23)?

By praising God. His prayer of verse 18 has been answered (v 19), and so prayer gives way to praise.

• What truths about God are we reminded of in these verses?

Daniel's praise offers us glimpses into the main themes of the whole book:

- There is a God of wisdom and power, who is in charge of time and of rulers (v 20-21).
- God graciously gives understanding to humans (v 21-22).
- This God is the God of Israel, of Daniel's "ancestors" (v 23).

9. What was the content of the dream (v 31-35)?

Daniel told the king that his troubling vision was of an image of a person, both enormous and awesome (v 31), made of gold at its top, then silver and bronze, and then iron, which was mixed with clay at its feet (v 32-33). Then a rock "struck the statue on its feet of iron and clay and smashed them" (v 34). The image is not only destroyed, but it disintegrates: "But the rock [literally, stone] that struck the statue became a huge mountain and filled the whole earth" (v 35).

10. What is the interpretation of the dream (v 36-45)?

Nebuchadnezzar—to whom God has given dizzying power, both in its breadth and depth (v 37-38)—is the "head of gold" (v 38). After him will come another, inferior kingdom—implicitly, this is the silver one, since a third, "bronze" kingdom will follow it (v 39). And fourthly, "there will be a fourth kingdom, strong as iron" which "smashes everything" (v 40). Strangely, though, this strongest of all kingdoms will also be made from clay—it will be "divided" (v 41), "partly strong and partly brittle" (v 42), and so it "will not remain united" (v 43).

Then comes the stone—and the stone represents a kingdom that "the God of heaven will set up ... that will never be destroyed" (v 44), that will supersede all the previous kingdoms. And the king, Daniel says, should be in no doubt that this vision will one day be reality; these things have been made known by "the great God," and so "the dream is true and its interpretation is trustworthy" (v 45).

11. Why would the words "after you" (v 39) have been a great relief to Nebuchadnezzar?

Because his kingdom would only be replaced after him, rather than during his watch. From our vantage point, we can recognize the subsequent kingdoms as likely being the Medo-Persians, the ancient Greeks, and the Romans. But they would happen after Nebuchadnezzar's reign—to use the image of the dream, the head would disintegrate, but not during the king's own reign. This dream is not meant to show Nebuchadnezzar that the sovereign God will smash him, but rather, to announce the good news of the king's continued kingdom, and of God's coming future kingdom.

12. What were the rise and fall of various powerful empires all heading toward (v 44-45)?

God's coming kingdom—a kingdom that would break the fourth earthly kingdom, fill the earth, and be established forever.

- **Read Luke 20:17-19. How does Jesus link the image of Daniel 2:44-45 to himself?**

  NOTE: It is important to realize that the NIV translation of "rock" is literally the word "stone."

  Jesus spoke these words in Luke 20 immediately after speaking a parable against those who refused to recognize him as the Messiah, the fulfillment of God's Old Testament promises. He likens their rejection of him to the killing of a vineyard owner's son and rightful heir by his rebellious tenants—and goes on to gather up a number of Old Testament "stone" references and apply them to himself.

After quoting from Psalm 118 directly, Jesus goes on to allude to Daniel 2: "Everyone who falls on that stone will be broken to pieces; anyone on whom it falls will be crushed" (Luke 20:18). In saying this at the end of a parable predicting his execution, Jesus is tying his own death to the stone that comes from heaven. He is the one "cut out … but not by human hands" (Daniel 2:45), which brings down all human kingdoms and ushers in the eternal kingdom of God. With the cross and resurrection comes the everlasting kingdom.

13. How is this both exciting for us and a warning to us?

If we are part of his kingdom, building our lives on the "stone" of the Lord Jesus, then we are part of an eternal kingdom that will never be replaced or defeated. There is no better realm to live in!

Equally, if deep down we are our own ruler, and refusing to submit to Jesus as our King, then we should be warned that we will one day be crushed by the "stone." No one can stand against God's eternal King: not the most mighty empires in the world's history, and certainly not us!

- **Remember that the meaning of the dream was intended for the pagan king, not the godly servant. What does this mean for us today?**

God sent the dream to the king (not to Daniel), because he had a word for the king, and through him for his empire. God wanted an audience with the world; and he still does today. Daniel is not only pointing us to Jesus; he is also an example to us—that we should boldly be stating to the world that God's wisdom is found in Jesus (1 Corinthians 1:21-25; Colossians 2:2-3). Daniel told the king that God was speaking to him, through the dream. We are to tell the world that God is speaking to them, through Jesus. The world needs people who understand and can clearly state God's word to the world. Wherever God has placed you, remember this: he has a word to be made known. He has placed you in a line of work where others need to hear your voice.

Faithful in the Fire

Daniel 3

The Big Idea

When we, like King Nebuchadnezzar, seek our own worship, we can rely on Jesus' perfect faithfulness for forgiveness. And when we, like Daniel's friends—and supremely the Lord Jesus—remain faithful in trials, God will see us through them.

Summary

Architecture is one way in which we seek to make our mark on the world, and let others know who we are and what we are capable of. In Daniel 3, King Nebuchadnezzar builds an image of gold of incredible dimensions (v 1), and demands all his subjects worship the image, on pain of death in his blazing furnace (v 4-6). He is setting up an idol in order to glorify himself.

When Daniel's three friends are accused of refusing to worship the image (v 8-12), they face a choice: faithfulness and the fire, or compromise and "safety." They choose the furnace (v 16-18), and yet God sees them through the furnace—they emerge completely unharmed (v 25-27). The fire the king intended for judgment is used by God as a fire of testing, refinement and salvation. (These are the two "uses" of fire in the Bible—see Explore More.) And the king comes to realize that, contrary to his expectations, there is one who has more authority than him, and who truly is sovereign over life and death—the God of Israel (v 28-29; see verse 15).

It is all too easy for us to stand outside this story in judgment over Nebuchadnezzar. We like to identify with the three courageous friends of Daniel. But this study encourages us to consider how we are like the king: how we like to call everyone within earshot to praise us, and how we seek to build things with our lives that will win us honor in the eyes of others. We promote the worship of idols instead of God.

As we shall see, the three friends point us primarily to Jesus. When tempted by the devil (Matthew 4:8-10), Jesus resisted the call to worship him, and the lure of power over kingdoms, in order to obey God: a decision that would ultimately lead him to his cross. Jesus is the supremely faithful, courageous man, and so is able to offer us forgiveness when we fail to worship God alone. And there is then, in Christ, the further application for us as his saved people to seek to remain faithful and joyful in our "fiery ordeals," as we see in 1 Peter 1 and 4: to be joyful, knowing that he will be with us and will bring us through, into our eternal inheritance.

Optional Extra

Print out or collect pictures of some famous (and not so famous) buildings in your country, or from throughout the world. Show them to your group; ask them to guess where they are, and what they are called, and then discuss what "message" the buildings are giving those who look at them. (Make sure there are a variety of "messages" in the buildings you choose.) This will lead you into the discussion in question 1.

Guidance for Questions

1. **What statements do people or organizations make through building impressive structures or buildings?**
We all have a deep desire to make our mark on the world. We want others to know who we are. One way to do that is to build something that makes a statement—that says, "This is how great/powerful/techno-logically capable we are" or "This is our outlook on life—how we see the world and how we want to be remembered by the world."

2. **What does Nebuchadnezzar make, and for what purpose?**
An image of gold (v 1), 90 feet (27m) high and only nine feet (3m) in circumference at its base—quite an architectural feat! It seems to have had three purposes:
   • To impress: the dimensions speak of aiming to impress and gain respect.
   • To celebrate: the guestlist in verses 2-3 for the day of dedication shows that its unveiling was an occasion of great celebration.
   • Most importantly, to be worshiped: everyone is commanded, when the music plays, to "fall down and

worship the image of gold" (v 5)—and they do (v 7). Failure to toe this new religious line would bring punishment—being "thrown into a blazing furnace" (v 6).

3. **In which verses do we see reference made to King Nebuchadnezzar and the words "set up"? What point is being made by this repetition?**
Verses 1, 2, 3, 5. (See also verses 12, 14, 18.) The king is setting up something meant to impress others and celebrate himself—to draw praise to himself as people worship his "image of gold." He appears to want to elevate himself to the level of a god. Compare 2:21, where Daniel proclaimed that God "deposes kings and raises up others." Here, Nebuchadnezzar is seeking to raise up himself.

4. **How does that now change (3:8-15)?**
"Some astrologers"—other prominent men in the king's service—accuse the trio (v 8). They recite the king's decree back to him (v 10), remind him of the punishment for failure to bow down to the statue (v 11), and then make their charge against the three Jews, who "neither serve your gods nor worship the image of gold you have set up."

The king's response to the accusation is "furious ... rage" (v 13). He asks the three Jews to defend themselves (v 14), and gives them a chance to comply with his decree (v 15). If they will, then "very good." But he repeats the punishment due for non-compliance (or rather, non-worship) too.

The three had been rewarded in Babylon as they remained faithful to God. But now, they learn that enjoying favor in Babylon—in the world—is rare for God's faithful people, and usually it is short-lived.

5. What choice do the three face?

Remaining faithful to God (and obedient to his commandments, see Exodus 20:3-6) by not worshiping an idol or the king, and facing the blazing, fiery furnace; or compromising on their faithfulness, worshiping an idol, and maintaining their lives and positions in the king's service.

6. What do they choose (v 16-18)?

Faithfulness and the fire: "We will not serve your gods or worship the image of gold you have set up" (v 18). They will face the furnace before they turn their back on their faith.

- **How are they answering the question the king asks them in verse 15?**

The king asked, "What god will be able to rescue you from my hand?" and his "blazing furnace" (v 15). The three answer by stating the truth that their God, the God of Israel, "is able to deliver us from it" (v 17). Notice that they do not presume that he will; but they believe that he can. It is as though they are saying, *You may think you are exalted, and have power over life and earth, but you are still just a man. We serve the God who does have that power.*

7. How can we (on a smaller scale) act as the king does in verses 1-7?

As with him, the architecture of our own soul rises to the heavens in self-adulation. And if given our way, we too are tempted to call upon everyone within earshot to pay their respects to our deeds. In our careers, relationships and purchases, and even in our service of our church, we are very easily motivated (at least partly) by a desire to look good, to earn praise and recognition from others, and to make our name great. We build lives that will earn the respect and praise of others.

Encourage your group to discuss how they find it tempting to do this in their own lives and circumstances.

8. Read Matthew 4:8-10. What are the similarities between Daniel 3 and this passage, and between the choice made by the three Jews and by Jesus?

- The three could have maintained their positions of power and influence with the king; Jesus was offered "all the kingdoms of the world and their splendor" by Satan (Matthew 4:8-9).
- Both the king and Satan demanded worship and submission (Matthew 4:9). They called the three friends, and the Lord Jesus, to "bow down and worship."
- Jesus, like the three, refused to compromise his faithfulness (Matthew 4:10).
- The three faced the furnace for

refusing to worship the king's image; Jesus, in choosing faithfulness and obedience to his Father, was ultimately choosing to go to the cross.

Explore More

○ *In the Bible, fire is associated with two things. Read Genesis 19:24; Revelation 19:20. What is the first association?*
Judgment. These are fires of destruction.

○ *Read Malachi 3:1-4; 1 Corinthians 3:11-15. What is the other?*
Refinement, testing, the revealing of what someone or something truly is. These are the fire of salvation.

○ *... when it comes to the king's fiery furnace, what kind of fire...*
○ *did he intend it to be?*
Judgment.

○ *did God use it to be?*
Testing, refinement and ultimately salvation. The faithfulness of the three was tested and found to be genuine; and God showed his power by saving them through the fire.

9. **How is the furnace described (v 19-22)? Why is this emphasized, do you think?**
The furnace is seven times hotter than usual (v 19): so hot that it kills the soldiers who take the three Jews to the entrance of the furnace (v 22).

The point being made is that Daniel's friends' deaths are absolutely certain. There is no way that they can survive the furnace.

• **So why do the three end up in the state they are in by verses 26-27?**
They come out alive, not even smelling of smoke, because, as the king sees "in amazement" (v 24), a fourth man appears in the fire with Shadrach, Meshach and Abednego—one who "looks like a son of the gods" (v 25). God rescues his people from the furnace.

NOTE: We are not told the identity of the fourth man. Some Christian readers are tempted to land hard on an assumption that he is a preincarnate Jesus, but it might be wise to be a bit more reserved. After all, it could just as easily have been an angel. We simply are not told.

10. **How does the king respond (v 28-30)?**
He praises "the God of Shadrach, Meshach and Abednego" for sending his angel to rescue his servants (v 28). Now it will be those who speak against the God of Israel who will face punishment, rather than those who refuse to worship anything other than that God (v 29).

• **What has changed in his view of himself? (Compare verses 4-5.)**
He had set up his great image in order to draw praise to himself, and he demanded absolute obedience (v 4-5). Now he recognizes that it is

the Jews' God who should be praised (v 28). He has begun to recognize his own place, great king though he is.

• **How has his view of the God of Israel changed? (Compare the end of verse 15.)**

He had been confident that no god could rescue men from his furnace (v 15). Now he knows that there is a God (and only one) that can "save in this way" (v 29).

11. **Read 1 Peter 4:12-14. What will happen as we live as God's people in this world?**

We will have many troubles and foes in this world. We will at times face a "fiery ordeal" where we have to choose between faithfulness and compromise, just as Daniel's friends did.

• **How should we view that?**

First, we should not be surprised. Second, we can rejoice, as we remember that God is with us, by his Spirit. He will be present with his own people, seeing us through.

12. **God brought these three believers through the fire. Read 1 Peter 1:3-9. In what sense do we know God will bring us through the "fire" of trials?**

Because he has given us an "inheritance that can never perish, spoil or fade" (v 4), and God's power is with us, shielding us until we reach salvation (v 5)—not shielding us from trials, but from giving in to those trials. This is what Peter says we need to know and believe even as we "suffer grief in all kinds of trials" (v 6), because, as we remain faithful, these fiery trials are fires of testing, proving, and refinement (v 7).

13. **What difference will believing this make...**

• **when we face the choice between compromise and faithfulness?**

We will choose to remain faithful, because we know that God will be with us, and will bring us through—even through death. We compromise and worship the things of the world when we forget that our God is with us, and powerful to rescue us, either from death or beyond death.

• **when we are in a trial because we are living faithfully?**

We will still be able to rejoice (a word Peter uses in both chapter 1 and chapter 4), because we know we "are receiving the end result of [our] faith, the salvation of [our] souls" (1:9). One of the greatest gifts to the Christian is the ability to rejoice in our relationship with God and our certainty about our future, even when we face grievous trials.

3

Humbled and Restored

Daniel 4

The Big Idea

The book of Daniel (and the whole Bible) is for public proclamation, offering individual people peace, as they come into God's eternal kingdom. God brings the proud—such as Nebuchadnezzar—low, in order to bring them into this kingdom.

Summary

In music, a melodic line is a short sequence of notes that forms the distinctive essence of a song. It is the part of the main melody that gets repeated and varied throughout. In the same way, the book of Daniel has a distinctive sound—something that gives it its own theme and richness of tone. And this kingly proclamation in the opening three verses of chapter 4 puts us on to it:

- It is public (v 1).
- It is personal (v 1-2).
- It is about God and his kingdom (v 3). Verses 1-3 leave us with the question: why is a pagan, powerful king making this public announcement? We discover this in the rest of the chapter. The king receives another dream, and again Daniel is given the task of interpreting it. In doing so, he tells the king that, powerful though he is, he will be brought low, stripped of all dignity, until he learns to acknowledge that the God of Israel is the one who is truly in control, and who gives all rulers their positions. As Daniel speaks truth to

power in this way, we learn great lessons for our own proclamation of the kingdom of God: that we must proclaim it with tender hearts and honest words, making clear the purpose of our message: that people need to humble themselves before God, giving up their pride and pretensions to autonomy so that they might come into his eternal kingdom.

Daniel's interpretation becomes reality in verses 28-33; and the king does indeed learn to look to heaven, and praise and glorify God rather than himself. (Compare his attitude in verses 29-30 and verses 34-37.) And in this way, he provides a dramatic portrayal of conversion, where we are humbled by God so that we are ready to be restored and lifted up by him.

Optional Extra

The early part of this study focuses on how 4:1-3 reveals the "melodic line" of the book—so begin your time together by listening to a couple of minutes of several pieces of music that have recurring melodies. (You could choose classical music, or music that is important to your country or culture, or pop music.) If you like, you could ask group members to see if they know each tune. Then play (in a different order) the songs/music again, but use different parts of the tune, asking group members to say the name of the piece of music as soon as they recognize it. They will probably recognize it via a recurring melody (or lyric).

Guidance for Questions

1. **What do people take pride in?**
   All sorts of things. Allow your group to come up with a variety of answers, encouraging them to think about themselves as well as others.

- **Can it ever be a good thing to lose what makes us proud? Why / how?**
  There is no wrong answer to this—you'll return to this idea, with reference to King Nebuchadnezzar, in question 11.

2. **Who is speaking here?**
   King Nebuchadnezzar.

- **Given what we have seen of him in Daniel 1 – 3, what is striking about his words in these verses?**
  We have seen Nebuchadnezzar conquering Jerusalem and taking items from its temple (1:1-2); and making an image that he commanded all people to worship, on pain of death (3:4-6). While we have also seen him recognizing that the God of Israel is real and powerful, and rescues, and should be praised (2:47; 3:28-29), now in 4:1-3 we find this powerful king speaking of what the Most High God has done for him, and exalting God's kingdom. These verses are much more personal and responsive than the king's previous announcements concerning the God of Daniel, Meshach, Shadrach, and Abednego.

3. **How is the king's message…**
- **something public?**
  It is a proclamation to everyone in his empire; in fact he wants it to be known by everyone everywhere (v 1). This is like a presidential address or a speech from the prime minister.

- **something personal? (Note: A better translation of the end of verse 1 is "Peace be multiplied to you!")**
  The king wants everyone to know about the "wonders that the Most High God has performed for me" (v 2). He wants to speak of God's personal kindness toward him. He has come to appreciate for himself not only that God is sovereign but that he offers salvation and peace, as seen in the declaration's opening greeting, which is best translated (as the ESV does), "Peace be multiplied to you" (v 1). His message is literally "gospel"—a royal announcement of good news.

- **centered on God and his kingdom?**
  The climax of the declaration is in verse 3, and it is about God's kingdom. The Most High God is establishing his forever kingdom upon the earth. As such, it will surpass every dominion this world has ever known. And not only that, but when God's kingly reign comes, it will be marked by signs and wonders of his gracious rule coming to people in personal ways. This work of God will endure from generation to generation.

  NOTE: This theme of God's kingdom is continually repeated throughout Daniel 4:

- "… so that the living may know that the Most High is sovereign over all kingdoms on earth and gives them to anyone he wishes" (v 17).
- "… until you acknowledge that the Most High is sovereign over all kingdoms on earth and gives them to anyone he wishes" (v 25).
- "… when you acknowledge that Heaven rules" (v 26).
- "… until you acknowledge that the Most High is sovereign over all kingdoms on earth and gives them to anyone he wishes" (v 32).
- "His dominion is an eternal dominion; his kingdom endures from generation to generation. All the peoples of the earth are regarded as nothing. He does as he pleases with the powers of heaven and the peoples of the earth. No one can hold back his hand or say to him: 'What have you done?'" (v 34-35).
- "Now I, Nebuchadnezzar, praise and exalt and glorify the King of heaven" (v 37).

4. What is the content of the dream (v 9-17)?

The king sees a great cosmic tree in the middle of the earth (v 10), which is visible throughout the world (v 11). It is both grand and good—it is described as having leaves that are beautiful and being laden with fruit that is abundant. It has enough fruit to feed the whole earth and enough foliage to shelter all the beasts of the field and the birds of heaven (v 12).

But then things take a darker turn. "A holy one, a messenger" comes bearing words (v 13-14). The book's first readers would have known this "messenger" was an angel. The message is this: the tree is to be chopped down, with all its glories stripped and scattered (v 14). The stump of that tree will remain; but it will be bound, and will be as an animal (v 15), with a mind to match (v 16). And all this will happen in order that "the living may know that the Most High is sovereign over all kingdoms on earth and gives them to anyone he wishes and sets over them the lowliest of people" (v 17)—that is, the fulfillment of this dream will fit the melodic line of Daniel.

- **How does it make the king feel (v 5)?**
  "Terrified."

5. Sum up Daniel's God-given interpretation of the dream in verses 24-27.

- v 24: It concerns the king.
- v 25: He will become like a wild animal, living "like the ox," until he accepts God's rule over the world and over him as king.
- v 26: Nebuchadnezzar will be restored when he acknowledges "that Heaven rules."
- v 27: The king needs to renounce his sins and live rightly and kindly in the hope that his prosperity might continue.

6. How do Daniel's words to the king show us…

• his love for the king (v 19)?

Daniel wants the content of the dream to refer to someone else, and the fallout from the dream to be transferred to them as well. In other words, he wishes that the content and the implications could be switched to someone else. He knew in fact that he could not change who the dream was about (v 17)—but these words are revealing his heart. Daniel wasn't one of those followers of God who seem to delight in the idea of the ungodly finally getting what they have coming to them from the hand of God—his heart was soft toward the king.

○ OPTIONAL: Read Luke 19:41-42. How do we see the same heart in Jesus?

He wept for those who were rejecting his coming rule—his heart broke over the judgment that was coming to them.

• his honesty?

Daniel does not shy away from telling the king that he is the subject of his own dream. He tells him, "Your Majesty, you are that tree!" (v 22)—that this decree has been "issued against my lord the king" (v 24), and that the king needs to respond by changing his attitude toward God and his conduct toward others (v 27). Remember who Daniel is speaking to—the most powerful human king in the world—and realize what incredible bravery he is showing in being so honest.

• God's purpose in all this (v 25-26)?

The punishment at hand had everything to do with Nebuchadnezzar's pride—his lack of recognition that the kingdom he ruled was the consequence of God's will (and not his own). God's purpose in breaking the king was to bring him to understand and accept that there was a King still greater than him, and humbly to praise and worship him.

7. Daniel is a believer in God, telling truth to an unbeliever. What does his example teach us about our own witness?

Refer back to question 6 and talk about whether…

• your hearts are tender toward those facing judgment.

• your words about the gospel are honest, and do not leave out the challenging or offensive aspects. We must be willing to tell others that God is not pleased with our pride—the human tendency to push him aside and think that we are the measure of all things. We must be willing to say why God works against people—so that we might one day know that he rules and we don't. Finally, we must be ready to call for repentance and offer hope.

• your witness includes both the challenge to repent and the hope that repentance will bring life (which is Daniel's thrust in verse 27).

Notice also that the text stops without telling us how the king responded on that day. The important thing to note is not how Daniel felt things went, nor how the king felt things had gone. Rather, we are meant simply to see that Daniel didn't shirk from speaking God's word into the life of the most powerful man in the world. In not doing so, he has provided us with an example of the backbone needed to be faithful when an opportunity comes.

8. **What was the king thinking as his humiliation arrived (v 29-30)?**
How much he had achieved, and how great his power and glory were. Pride was guiding his thoughts and words. Notice the personal pronouns: "The great Babylon *I* have built ... by *my* mighty power and for the glory of *my* majesty." Nebuchadnezzar's heart was heralding that Babylon was his city, standing as a monument to his glory.

9. **Whose words were more powerful and accurate: the king's or heaven's?**
Heaven's! The king was about to discover that he was not mighty or majestic.

10. **What are we being taught about human achievements and pride in such things?**
Essentially, that Daniel's words in verse 17 are true: that it is God who gives people their positions (even kings); he gives us all we have, and he can take it away again. In other words, our achievements are really all God's

(he gives us the life, the abilities, the circumstances, and the energy that we use to achieve or accumulate); so we should not praise ourselves or seek our own glory through them.

Note that verse 17 adds that God gives kingship to the lowly. This is seen most of all in how God has exalted his Son, who lived in human flesh, in great humility, even unto death (see Philippians 2:5-11).

11. **What did Nebuchadnezzar do, and what then happened (v 34, 36)?**
He raised his "eyes toward heaven" (v 34); and his sanity, honor and splendor were all restored to him.

12. **What had this powerful king now learned to do (v 34-35, 37)?**
To praise God, and to give him honor and glory (instead of himself). He put pen to paper in search of words that would convey his heart's new desire to worship the true and living God. He had not merely returned to his previous state; he had broken through to a mindset that was moved to praise God publicly and personally. We need to read his words remembering that this is the man who ruled the greatest empire in the known world, who had invaded and destroyed Jerusalem, and who had cast Daniel's friends into the fiery furnace; and yet who was now humble before the Most High God, knowing that he is the greatest ruler, he has the greatest power, his kingdom is eternal, and his ways are right and just.

- **Why was it a good thing for the king to lose everything that he had achieved and to be utterly humiliated?**

  Because it allowed him to break through into true submission to and praise of God—to come into his kingdom. He ends up in a better place not only in terms of his earthly position (v 36) but in his spiritual position, for he no longer glories in himself but in the "King of heaven."

13. **How is Nebuchadnezzar's experience here a very dramatic picture of what happens in every conversion?**

    When someone puts their faith in Christ as their Ruler and Rescuer, they cease to seek and take glory for themselves, and exchange that for giving glory to God. They acknowledge that life does not revolve around them and is not all about them; there is one greater than them. They stop seeking to rule themselves and submit to the rule of the King of heaven, living in a kingdom where they are not sovereign, but a subject. The pronouns of I and my, me and mine, must be replaced with "you, God" and "yours, God."

- **Share some examples of God breaking someone's pride in order to bring them to worship and praise him—either from your own life or from those of others you know.**

  Be ready to share your own story, and those of others you have witnessed to or seen coming to faith.

Explore More

- **Read Luke 22:31-34, 54-62. How do we see God breaking another man's pride in his own abilities so that he might come to truly love and follow the Lord Jesus?**

  The apostle Peter was very sure of his own abilities to follow Jesus and stand courageously for him. The Lord predicted his failure and allowed him to fail in just that way: denying his Lord at Jesus' moment of greatest personal need. Peter needed to weep bitter tears of failure before he could come to acknowledge his dependence on Christ, and his work and prayers, and to then be able to serve Christ's people.

- **How does this both humble and comfort us?**

  Like Peter, we need to realize that we are utterly dependent on God—that his word is true, not ours; and that it is his work for us, not ours for him, that we rely on. But it is comforting to know that when we fail, Jesus did not and does not fail—he went to the cross even as Peter denied him, and he went to the cross for us, too, so that he might forgive us and change us.

4

Who Rules? Kings vs. God

Daniel 5 - 6

The Big Idea

Daniel shows his trust in God by refusing the gifts of this world, speaking truth to power, being blameless in his work, and obeying God even when his life is in danger. This is how we, too, show that we know the God who, in Jesus, was himself condemned to die, only to live beyond that place of death.

Summary

This study takes in two of the most famous episodes in the entire book: the writing on the wall, and Daniel in the lions' den. They are both reasonably straightforward in their details, and have much to teach us not only about how we as believers are called to live as God's people, but also in pointing us to the ultimate courage and faithfulness of the Lord Jesus.

In his interaction with Belshazzar, we see Daniel…

- refusing to accept his offer of possessions and power.
- speaking truth to power (just as he had to Nebuchadnezzar during his reign).

And in his dealings with King Darius, we witness him…

- being such a useful, incorruptible, wise administrator that Darius wishes to set him over the entire kingdom; and Daniel's enemies cannot find any part of his conduct that can be accused of wrongdoing.

- praying to God, as was his custom, despite Darius having issued a decree commanding no one to pray to anyone other than him.
- being willing to go into the lions' den (and what should have been certain death) rather than compromise his obedience to the God of the Bible (just like his friends when faced with the blazing furnace).

Daniel's conduct is put into sharp contrast with those around him: the hubristic Belshazzar, seeking to proclaim his power over the God of Israel even as Darius invades his capital city; the envious administrators who plot to pit Daniel's loyalty to God against his service of the king, and so aim to bring him down; and the weakness of the king, who is tricked into condemning his favorite servant to death.

But more than showcasing the righteousness of Daniel, these chapters reveal the power and goodness of God—the God who judges even kings when they refuse to humble themselves before him and instead seek to hold him in their hand; and the God who is powerful to save his people from death.

Optional Extra

Ask one or more group members to research the lives of Christian martyrs, who went to their deaths rather than compromise their obedience to God. Ask them to present, in a couple of minutes each, the life and death of that martyr, and lead into a discussion of what it was that inspired and enabled them to give up their lives for their faith.

Guidance for Questions

1. **How can you tell that someone trusts in God?**

   There are many good answers to this question—make sure your group realise that real trust will show itself in our actions and conduct in the world, as well as our confession of faith in church. You could return to this question at the end of the study.

2. **Write down in three or four sentences a summary of the events of the chapter, and what you think the meaning of it is for us.**

   Your group may or may not mention all of the following important details:
   - King Belshazzar holds a great feast in honor of his gods (v 1), and he calls for Israel's gold drinking vessels, which had been used for worship in the Jerusalem temple, to be brought; the partygoers drink from them, praising their gods (v 3-4).
   - A hand appears, and writes on the wall (v 5); no one can decipher the writing, but the queen remembers that Daniel had great understanding, and he is summoned (v 7-13).
   - The king offers Daniel the third most prominent position in the kingdom (v 16), but Daniel turns this down (v 17), criticizes the king

for his refusal to humbly acknowledge God as Nebuchadnezzar had, and says that the writing on the wall means the king has been counted and found wanting, and so his kingdom will fall. Sure enough, that night Belshazzar is killed and his kingdom is conquered by Darius the Mede (v 30-31).

The meanings your group members draw at this stage will vary, and there are many right answers. The aim is not to make sure everyone is right, but to encourage them to think for themselves about what the narrative is telling us.

3. **What is the king trying to prove by his actions in verses 2-4, do you think?**

   That he has power over Israel, and over their God—so the king can now use items fashioned for worship of the Creator in his drunken revelry. It is as though he clenches his fingers around the God of Israel as he holds his cup. He wants everyone to know that he owns Yahweh.

4. **What should Belshazzar have known to do, and why (v 22)?**

   He should have known to humble his heart and acknowledge the authority of the God of Israel, because he "knew all" (v 22) about how his "father Nebuchadnezzar" (v 18—this does not mean literally his father, but rather his ancestor) had been humbled so that he would acknowledge God. He should have known better than to think he could hold

God in his hand; but instead he has "not humbled [him]self" (v 22).

- **How does God respond, both in what he promises and in what happens (v 28, 30)?**

God promises through Daniel that his judgment is coming: that the kingdom will be divided and given to others (v 28). And that very night, Babylon fell, Belshazzar was killed, and Darius the Mede came to power (v 30-31).

5. **Daniel knew the Lord's verdict when he refused the king's offer (v 16-17). How would knowing how things would play out affect his perspective on what the king was offering?**

The king, desperate to know the meaning of the writing on the wall, stammers out promises to Daniel of bling, a shawl, and a share of his power. But Daniel knew that they would soon not be his to give. They sounded like wonderful gifts, but they were temporary. Daniel knew this, and so he was unimpressed by them (v 17).

6. **How does this warn us about the pride in our own hearts?**

We find it very easy to think we can control God, or pursue our own pleasure while ignoring his rule. It is the nature of the human heart to "neither [glorify] him as God nor [give] thanks to him" (Romans 1:21). We need to be honest with ourselves about ways in which we seek to "hold God in our hand"; if we do not repent of it, we will be found wanting, and stand on the threshold of judgment. Human pride is serious.

- **How does it teach us to view this world?**

Daniel was not impressed by the king's feast, nor by his offer of presents and power, because he knew that it was passing. This was a powerful king, but his end was coming. We need to remember that whatever we may accumulate now, we will leave it all behind upon death; and so will everyone else. So we will not live grasping for what we can get now; we will seek instead to obey God, and look forward to eternity with him. And we will not be envious of those who have possessions or power but do not know God, any more than Daniel was envious of Belshazzar.

7. **Write down in three or four sentences a summary of the events of the chapter, and what you think the meaning of it is for us.**

- Daniel rises to dizzying heights in Darius' service (v 1-3), but his enemies at court convince the king to decree on pain of death that all must pray to him, and no one else (v 6-9).
- Daniel nevertheless prays publicly toward Jerusalem (v 10), and is arrested and accused (v 11-15).
- He is thrown into the lions' den (v 16-17), but God sends an angel to ensure he is not harmed (v 19-22).
- Instead, his enemies are thrown to the lions (v 24), and the king comes

to praise the God of Israel, who is able to rescue his people (v 25-27).

8. **What is striking about the only way Daniel's enemies can find a reason to accuse him (v 4-5)?**

They were "unable" to "find grounds for charges against Daniel in his conduct of government affairs"—there was "no corruption in him" (v 4). His books were in order; his numbers all added up. No bribes had been taken and witnesses to the contrary could not be found. And so it was determined that if they had any chance of successfully bringing Daniel down, they would need to pit his fidelity to God against his faithfulness to the king (v 5). There was nothing in Daniel's work that could be criticized—nothing. Even his enemies could find nothing offensive, other than his resolve to obey God.

• **Why were they so determined to bring him down, do you think?**

Almost certainly, they were motivated by envy. The king was about to promote a foreigner over Persians, a man of exile over those born into and raised within the indigenous nobility. Notice how they point out to the king that Daniel is "one of the exiles from Judah" (v 13).

9. **How do verses 10-15 contrast the resolute courage of Daniel and the weakness of the king?**

Daniel continues to pray "just as he had done before" (v 10), even though it now risks his life. The king, on the

other hand, comes off as weak. He has been trapped by his advisers into condemning his own favored servant to death, and is powerless, try as he might, to prevent Daniel being thrown to the lions (v 14-15).

10. **In what sense is Daniel's God, as well as Daniel himself, on trial (v 16)?**

The king raises the question of whether or not Daniel's God has the power to save his people from death. So he is basing his view of the God of Israel on what happens to this Israelite exile in the lions' den.

11. **So what does Daniel's rescue reveal about…**

• **God (v 20-22, 26-27)?**

Daniel's God was shown to be the living, powerful God—the God of Israel was vindicated. He was also seen to be the God who rescues and saves (v 27), and so is worthy of fear and reverence (v 26).

• **Daniel (v 22-23)?**

Daniel had done nothing wrong—he grounds his deliverance in his innocence before both God and the king.

Explore More

○ *Imagine you were one of the 122 who had successfully accused Daniel. Trace how well or badly things are going for you through the chapter. Then put yourself in Daniel's position and do the same thing. You could give your group—in pairs, individually, or all together—a piece* of paper with a graph drawn on, the horizontal axis representing the passage of time, and the vertical axis how well/badly Daniel's accusers/ Daniel are doing. Of course, things start well for Daniel and less well for his accusers, then go well for the accusers and terribly for Daniel, and finally (and suddenly) turn out really well for Daniel and even more terribly for his accusers.

○ **How does this teach us, as God's people, to view life, opposition, and times when those who oppose God's people thrive?**
The men who disdained Daniel and his God faced the judgment they had prepared for Daniel. We are being warned against rejecting Daniel's God, for there is no hope of pres- ervation outside him. They thought they had triumphed, but found them- selves utterly defeated. Daniel, on the other hand, seemed powerless and certain to die, but ended up prospering throughout the reign of Darius (v 28). What matters in life is our relationship with God, not how well or badly things are going. If you have time, read Psalm 73.

---

12. **What similarities do you see between Daniel in chapter 6 and Jesus in the Gospels?**
Jesus was also…
• innocent.
• falsely accused.

• let down by a weak ruler who failed to protect him (Pontius Pilate).
• delivered over to death.
• vindicated by being delivered from death (though unlike Daniel, he ac- tually died).
• displayed the existence, power, and mercy of God in his experience.

13. **What flaws do we see in those around Daniel in these two epi- sodes?**
The hubristic pride of Belshazzar. The envy of the other satraps. The weak- ness of the king.

• **How does Daniel show us what it means to believe in the sovereign, saving God of the Bible?**
It means not setting too much store by the things of this world; being willing to speak truth to power, even at risk to ourselves; being blameless in our conduct; and being willing to obey God even if it leads to death.

• **Discuss what these flaws, and this faithfulness, would look like in your particular culture and settings today.**
This is an opportunity for your group to be specific in terms of how the faithfulness Daniel shows might look in their own lives. Encourage them to talk about their own walk with God as well as that of others. And remind your group that when we fail, we look to Jesus, the faithful one who died and rose to offer his righteousness to us.

5

One Like a Son of Man

Daniel 7

The Big Idea

God's kingdom—ruled by the Son of Man, Jesus—will prevail and defeat ungodly earthly kingdoms; but life will be hard for his people until that day comes.

Summary

Daniel 7:1 marks a shift in the book of Daniel, in four ways. First, the genre changes from historical narrative to apocalyptic literature. The simplest definition of the word *apokalypsis* is "revelation" (which is why the last book of the Bible bears that title). As such, this genre is an unveiling—a pulling back of the curtain on the unseen transcendent world and its role in bringing this present world to an end. I don't want you to be frightened off by Daniel 7 – 12 or believe that you have no chance of understanding it! Aim to be a confident and expectant reader. Under the guidance of the Holy Spirit, I am convinced that there are gospel truths here—in picture form— that will be readily understood if we simply take a good look at the "movie" God has provided.

Second, the book no longer proceeds chronologically; the four visions in chapters 7 – 12 take place during events that have already happened, in chapters 4 – 6.

Third, in 7:1 we are told that a vision was given to Daniel. To this point, Daniel has only served as interpreter to the dreams of others; he explained God's word to the rulers of this world, but now it is the man of God himself that God wants as his audience. These visions are primarily for the church, rather than the world.

Fourth, whereas chapters 1 – 6 are court tales that help us to see what it means for God's people to make their home in "Babylon"—in a world that does not know God—now these visions will reveal what is required in getting home from Babylon: the path believers must take in order to reach glory with God. (Daniel would discover that the Jews' return to Jerusalem from exile would not be the moment when all God's promises would be fulfilled.)

This study takes in the first vision, in chapter 7. It contains themes that will be repeated in the other three visions: that human kingdoms will rise and fall, but that God is sovereign over all of them, will judge and overthrow those who oppose him, and will establish his own, everlasting kingdom, where his people will at last dwell in peace. And 7:13-14 reveals that God's kingdom will be ruled by "one like a son of man"—whom the Gospels reveal to be Jesus. This study suggests that these verses in Daniel 7 regarding that son of man are pointing us to the ascension of the crucified, risen Christ, when he defeated the ungodly kingdoms of this world and received all power and the right to demand allegiance from all.

Optional Extra

Before you start to study the passage in detail and work through the questions below, give your group members a piece of paper each, read the passage through, and ask them to draw the vision.

Guidance for Questions

1. **What do you think your life as a Christian will be like between now and the day you die or when Jesus returns? Why do you think this?**

This question is designed to encourage your group to think about whether life as a follower of God will be essentially good, comfortable, etc. or essentially hard. In the West, it is easy to assume that we might be able to live both Christianly and comfortably. So the second part of the question is designed to see where people's ideas about the Christian life are drawn from. Daniel 7 will give us a clear, if unsettling answer. Questions 11-12 return to this theme.

2. **This time the dream comes to Daniel, and not to the king (v 1). Why is that significant?**

Daniel, the man of God, is the one God wants as his audience. (And, as we will see, he will now be the one who needs an interpreter—v 19.) This change signals a shift in the intended audience. The focus in the first six chapters was on a word God wanted proclaimed to the outside world. As such, God revealed himself to various kings, but always in a way that required Daniel to preach to them. Now, with Daniel becoming the recipient of visions instead, we are to understand that the last six chapters will focus on the word God wanted proclaimed to his own people. He speaks to Daniel and, by him, to Israel—and to us as God's people today.

3. **What does Daniel see in this dream (v 2-8)?**

"Four great beasts" coming up out of the sea (v 2-3). You might like to share with your group that in the Bible, as well as in later Greco-Roman literature, a body of water like this is a place of chaos: the place where evil rules, and from where doers of evil emerge from the filthy deep (see, for example, Revelation 13:1; 21:1). Here in Daniel 7, God is stirring up the deep, and controlling the very things that are actively rising in opposition to him.

- The first beast (v 4) is like a lion with an eagle's wings.
- The second (v 5) is like a bear.
- The third (v 6) is like a winged leopard, with four heads.
- The fourth (v 7-8) is "different"—it is described only as having "large iron teeth" and "ten horns."

- **Read verse 17. What do these beasts represent?**

Each is a symbol, representing a kingdom.

4. **Read Revelation 13:1-3. What do you notice about this symbolic description of Rome? What does this tell you about what the symbols in Daniel 7 stand for more generally?**

It is a composite beast of the four we have in Daniel 7. So in this apocalyptic vision given to the apostle John, all four images refer to a single kingdom: Rome. While the beasts rising out of the great sea can be identified with the successive kingdoms of Babylon, Medo-Persia, Greece, and Rome, these ungodly icons cross over barriers of time and space. And as they run through the centuries, they can be identified with various kingdoms that oppose God. They can stand for all earthly kingdoms or political entities that oppose God.

5. **After the rise of the fourth beast, what happens next (v 9-10)?**

The "Ancient of Days" (a figure who is ageless) takes his throne—a symbol of rule and authority. He sits to make judgment (v 10). In verses 9b-10, he is described as pure—the dominant image is of fire, which (as we saw in study 2) both purifies and judges.

- **What does the Ancient of Days do (v 11-12)?**

He judges the great fourth beast, even while the beast is busily boasting of his power (v 11). The judgment is that he is killed and destroyed. The other beasts have their power taken away, though they continue to be present as shadows of their more powerful selves (v 12).

6. **Who does Daniel see next (v 13-14)? Where is this person, and what is he given?**

Daniel sees "one like a son of man" (v 13). He is approaching the Ancient of Days, to be given an everlasting kingdom that includes rule over all peoples, nations, and languages.

- **Read Mark 14:53, 60-64. Who is the "one like a son of man" whom Daniel saw?**

According to Jesus, it is Jesus himself! And notice the moment at which Jesus chooses to make this claim; it is as he stands on trial for his life. He has nothing to gain from identifying with the Son of Man (as the court's reaction shows).

- **Read Philippians 2:8-11. When did he approach the Ancient of Days to receive universal power and authority?**

Daniel 7:13-14 is often read as a description of what will happen to Jesus at the end of human history. But it makes more sense to understand it as having already occurred, at the time of the Lord's ascension. Philippians 2 tells us that, after his obedient death on the cross (v 8), God "exalted [past tense] him to the highest place." In the death, resurrection, and ascension of Jesus, the kingdoms of this world were defeated, albeit with the shadow of their power existing for a prolonged season; and Jesus entered into the heavens, stood before the Ancient of Days, and received a kingdom that demanded the allegiance of all peoples, nations, and languages. This was the moment when he sat down at the right hand of the Father, and began to reign. Do pause to praise him in your group at this point, and to acknowledge before him this wonderful reality.

Explore More

○ *Read Psalm 2. How does this psalm also refer to the themes that Daniel sees in his vision?*
- *The nations conspire against, and use all their power to oppose, God (v 1-3).*
- *God sits on his throne and laughs (v 4).*
- *He rebukes and pours out his wrath on the kingdoms by installing his King, his Son (v 5-7).*
- *This King defeats the nations (v 8-9) and offers refuge to his people (v 12).*

7. **Every worldly power (the "beasts") looked extremely strong and irresistible to Daniel—and they still do to us today. What does Daniel 7:9-10 remind us of?**
A succession of ungodly kingdoms will rise up against heaven—but will not succeed. These kingdoms will strut upon the world's stage; but righteousness will prevail because God has won and will win. Living after Christ's ascension, we know that the Son of Man is already ruling with all power and authority. The

strongest of earthly states cannot stand against him.

- **How should this affect how we respond to news about oppressive political systems, and to the ungodly demands of our own rulers?**
We should not be surprised, nor should we despair. We should take heart—our King reigns, and has defeated and will defeat all other pretenders to his authority. We can continue to obey him (just as Daniel and his friends did in chapters 1 – 6), knowing that he sits on his throne in heaven.

8. **How would verses 17-18 have encouraged him?**
God's people will "receive the kingdom and will possess it forever" (v 18). So Daniel is being told that while ungodly and arrogant kings will continue to succeed one another on the world's stage, he does not need to be anxious and alarmed, because God will see to it that his people will receive his everlasting kingdom. The end is already guaranteed, and it is good news for God's people.

9. **How does that explanation leave him feeling (v 28)?**
"Deeply troubled"—it made him turn pale.

- **Why would verses 23-25 have made him feel like that?**
Because there he learned that the fourth beast would have virtually universal power, which it would use destructively (v 23). Then one "horn"

(a symbol associated with strength), i.e. a king, would arise (v 24), and he would oppress God's people, who would be delivered into his hands (v 25—a better translation is the ESV's: he will seek to "wear out the saints of the Most High"). A terrible time for God's people lay ahead.

NOTE: Who is this king? This has been a point of great contention! For those who hold that the fourth beast in this chapter refers to Rome, it may be identified with the destruction of Jerusalem around AD 70, when Titus, a Roman general, mocked Israel's holy site by worshiping Roman deities at the Jerusalem temple.

However, for those who separate out the kingdoms of the Medes and the Persians, the fourth beast becomes Greece rather than Rome, which leads them to see this horn as Antiochus Epiphanes, who ruled Greece from 175 BC until his death in 164. This ruler was known for escalating rhetoric against the Most High, going so far as to introduce coins which stated of himself, "God Manifest."

Still other interpreters believe that this horn has yet to come on the scene: that he is a future "antichrist." But we must get used to the idea that in this genre, visions consistently collapse one epoch in time upon another. Images or figures can apply to more than one period in history. This should keep us from becoming overly rigid. This horn could stand for one or both of Titus and Antiochus Epiphanes, and for others in history (and the future) who seek to break God's people.

10. How is this dream in Daniel 7 (and particularly this last explanation) reshaping his expectations?

A long and arduous road lay ahead, even though deliverance lay at the end of it. Horrific things would happen to God's people—incredibly difficult future days would come.

11. How should Daniel's dream reshape our expectations of...

- **our future between today and the day Jesus returns?**

Life will be hard, and sometimes incredibly difficult, for God's people today. Being members of God's kingdom now does not mean our lives will be more comfortable—it will make them less comfortable.

- **our future beyond the day Jesus returns?**

Life will be glorious as we live in righteousness and peace under the perfect established rule of the Lord Jesus.

12. What difference will having a Daniel-7 perspective of our present and our future make, day by day?

We will live without despair, and we will live with hope. We will not be surprised or crushed when things go wrong, nor will we grow too accustomed to things going well. Our hope will be in the future, rather than in the present. We will be able joyfully to obey God even when that comes at great cost, since we know where this world, and we as his people, are heading. We will live knowing that the Ancient of Days, and not the kingdoms of this world, has the last word.

13. **What will go wrong if we forget...**
- **what life is like for God's people as they travel through life toward home in God's kingdom?**
  We may...
  - compromise on obedience when it is hard.
  - grow bitter with God for not

providing us with a life that he has never promised us in the present.

- **what life is like for God's people once they reach their home in God's kingdom?**
  We may give up on our faith, thinking that it is not worth the cost, and/or that an ungodly pursuit of the things of this world will deliver more to us than an obedient pursuit of the kingdom of God.

6

Daniel's Prayer

Daniel 8 - 9

The Big Idea

Daniel gives an example of prayer prompted by a biblical worldview and reading God's word that drives us to confess sins and to plead for mercy, based on God's character—and Daniel is also a shadow of the Lord Jesus, who prays for his people today.

Summary

The second vision, in chapter 8, repeats many of the themes of the first, albeit through different imagery—a ram (the Medo-Persian Empire) followed by a goat (representing the Greek empire). This time, though, there are more details of

how hard life will be for God's people in the "Beautiful Land" (v 9), and how a king who will arise from the Greek Empire—almost certainly Antiochus Epiphanes (who ruled from 175 to 164 BC)—will oppose and almost destroy God's people.

This study also takes in chapter 9, where Daniel turns to prayer. In his prayer, we see...

- his understanding of God's righteous, powerful, and merciful character.
- his humility in confession, and his identification in confession with the whole people of God and their sin and rebellion against God (and in seeing this, we are pointed to Jesus,

who identified with God's sinful people to the extent of dying for them on the cross, and is now interceding for them at the right hand of God, Romans 8:34).

• his petition based on God's mercy, and in light of his confidence that God will keep his promises.

Daniel is still praying when the angel Gabriel arrives to further explain the vision of Daniel 8—his prayers are answered even while he is praying them. There is much here to encourage us—both the wonderful truth that the Lord Jesus is praying for us as his people and that our own prayers are heard in heaven!

Optional Extra

Print out pictures of a range of animals and ask your group to discuss which would win in a head-to-head fight. This links to the vision in terms of God giving Daniel animal symbols to represent the kingdoms—and is also good fun!

Guidance for Questions

1. Why do we pray? What stops us from praying?

There will be many answers to both questions. In this study (and especially in the second half), we will see various reasons why God's people pray, which will help us resist the temptation not to do so. Question 13 refers back to this question.

2. Describe the vision Daniel sees in verses 2-12. (You may like to draw it.)

It takes place 200 miles to the east of Babylon, in the citadel of Susa, next to the Ulai canal (v 2)—i.e. in the realm of the Persians. So Daniel is being taken to see the future.

Verses 3-4 describe a ram, in such a way that its horns are meant to leave the biggest impression. Verse 4 gives us a sense of the extent of the power given to this ram (or nation).

Then, in verses 5-7, a goat appears, galloping at such speed that its feet never seem to touch the ground (v 5), and goring the ram to death (v 6-7). The goat stands in the ram's place. But then the goat's horn is broken, and four "prominent horns" replace it (v 8).

Out of one of these four horns then grows another horn (v 9), which begins small, but grows in power toward the south and east and the "Beautiful Land." (Explain to your group that this almost certainly refers to Israel—to the land promised to Abraham, Isaac, and Jacob by God.)

3. What will the "horn" do in the "Beautiful Land" (v 11-12, 23-25)?

• v 11-12: He will fight against those who dwell in Israel; the temple will once more be overrun, and the daily sacrifices halted. Truth will be trampled, and the horn will grow still stronger.

• v 23-25: He will "destroy ... the holy people" (v 24); deceit will prosper, and there will be great destruction (v 25).

• How will things end up (v 14, 25)?

This horn, powerful and destructive though he is, will not win. The sanctuary (in the Jerusalem Temple) will be "reconsecrated" (v 14)—that is, used for the sacrifices God had purposed it for—and, as the horn fights against the "Prince of princes," he will be defeated—not by human power but by divine power (v 25).

4. **Read John 2:19-22; Hebrews 10:11-14. In what sense was Jesus the final fulfillment of Daniel 8:14?**
Jesus is the ultimate "reconsecration" of the temple, because he himself is the temple: the way that God is present with his people, and the means by which his people can approach God. And Jesus is the ultimate sacrifice—by means of his blood, he won forgiveness once and for all. So after his death on the cross, there are no more sacrifices—not because God's enemies are preventing them from being offered but because there is no need for them to be offered.

5. **How does this vision once again underline the way God's people need to look at their present and their future?**
God's people should expect a season of suffering before ultimately being delivered. God's enemies will fight and destroy, but they will not win. In this sense, the message of Daniel 8 is the same as that of Daniel 7 (and we need to hear it again, for we need repeatedly to have our expectations reshaped). Daniel 8 also reminds us to be thankful to Christ and continue to praise him, even in present trials,

because his substitutionary death and resurrection have secured our ultimate deliverance. For Daniel, this lay in the future; for us, it is a matter of historical record.

6. **What prompted Daniel's prayer (9:2-3)?**
His prayer was offered in response to his private reading of and meditation on God's word. (And, given that this chapter follows two visions which revealed to Daniel how long and arduous the road home from Babylon would be, it is likely that he was also praying in light of the worldview he had been given.)

• **Read Jeremiah 29:10-14. Why is it strange that Daniel responds in "sackcloth and ashes"—clothes that signify an attitude of mourning (Daniel 9:3)?**
Because Jeremiah 29 indicated to Daniel the nearness of the end of the physical exile of God's people. Daniel was likely taken into exile around 605 BC (Babylon then repeatedly attacked Jerusalem for two decades until it finally fell in 586 BC); and verse 1 places chapter 9 in about 539 BC. So the 70 years of exile are almost over. So it is strange that Daniel responds by fasting and wearing clothes of mourning, or repentance.

7. **How does 9:4-16 show why Daniel dressed like this?**
Daniel repeatedly confesses in these verses that "we have sinned" (v 5, 8, 11—see the same confession put

differently in verses 6, 7, 9-10, 13). He was confident that God would keep his promises—but he also knew the reality of the people God had made his promise to. A confidence in God does not mean we can complacently ignore our sin.

8. But Daniel himself was "innocent in [God's] sight" (6:22). What does his identification with all God's people, and his confession as a member of that people, teach us about our prayers?

We stand before God not only as individuals, but as members of his people. So we should confess our people's sinfulness, not only our own. We should identify so deeply with other believers, as one people, that their sin becomes our problem (just as their obedience becomes our joy). Our prayers should be offered for our church and God's people as a whole, not only for ourselves.

9. On what basis does Daniel dare to plead to God to keep his promises (9:17-19)?

"For your sake" (v 17, 19)—and "because of your great mercy" (v 18). Daniel asks God to act for his own sake and glory, not based on his people's righteousness.

○ **OPTIONAL: What other things could he have based his plea on? Why would these have been insufficient?**

Verse 18: "We do not make requests of you because we are righteous." His confidence does not rest in the godliness of his people (he has confessed that they have not been godly), nor in their ability to make a fresh start with God (for he knows they will not be able to live in full obedience).

10. We have seen the innocent Daniel praying on behalf of God's people. Read Romans 8:34; 1 John 2:1. How is he picturing what Jesus is doing for us right now?

The risen Lord Jesus is interceding for us at the right hand of God. Right now, he is praying to his Father on our behalf. And he is speaking to God about our sins, and pleading his own righteousness and atoning death on our behalf. He identified with his people in his death (see 2 Corinthians 5:21); and now he identifies with us as he speaks to his Father for us.

Explore More

○ **Read Ezra 1:2-4, 64-67. How did God both keep his promise of Jeremiah 29 and answer Daniel's prayer?**

Cyrus (moved by God) allowed the Jews to return to Jerusalem, and to rebuild the temple—and commanded the other people of his great empire to assist the Jews in this endeavor. And so over 42,000 returned (though Daniel, as chapter 10 makes clear, was not among them— perhaps because by this stage, he was very old).

11. **Who appears, when, and why (v 20-23)?**
    - The angel Gabriel appears (v 21).
    - He appears while Daniel is praying, confessing, and "making my request to the LORD my God for his holy hill" (i.e. for Jerusalem to be restored—v 20).
    - He has come "to give [Daniel] insight and understanding" (v 22).

12. **But, when the time finally comes, what will happen (v 24)?**
    - Transgression will finish.
    - Sin will end.
    - Wickedness will be atoned for.
    - Everlasting righteousness will be brought in.
    - The vision and prophecy will be sealed up.
    - The Most Holy Place will be anointed.

    - **How is this pointing us toward Jesus—both his death and resurrection, and his return—as the final fulfillment?**

    It was Jesus' work on the cross that finished the transgression and put an end to all our sin. It was his death that atoned for our wickedness and gave his people everlasting righteousness. It was his work that fulfilled ("seal up") both the vision and the prophet. It was his blood shed that established him as the Most Holy Place, where God's people are able to approach the holy God. We therefore find one fulfillment of this prophecy in Christ's death and resurrection. And those who also look beyond that to the second coming of Christ should not be ruled out of bounds either; for at his return, there will be no more sin, his people will be righteous, and we will all live in the full presence of God (see Revelation 21:22).

Explore More

○ **Reread Daniel 9:25-27. Can you trace out four stages that will take place?**
   - *The restoration and rebuilding of Jerusalem, and the arrival of an Anointed One to accomplish it (v 25).*
   - *The building gets underway, but is met with trouble (v 25).*
   - *The Anointed One is put to death (or more literally, "cut off") (v 26).*
   - *Destruction returns to Jerusalem and its temple (v 26).*

---

13. **How have these chapters encouraged you about why God's people pray? Look back at your answer to question 1. Which of the reasons why we find prayer hard can Daniel 8 – 9 help us with?**

    We pray because it is the only right response to knowing what the present for God's people's is like, and what our future will be like; and to reading God's word, where we learn of his great promises. So we pray confidently, but we also make prayers of confession, and petition God in light of his character and promises revealed in his word. And we pray because we know that prayer is answered, just as Daniel's was (though often not as quickly, nor by an angelic visitation!).

Below are some reasons why Christians find prayer hard, and how these chapters help:

- *The world seems out of control:* Daniel 8 reminds us this is not a sign that things are wrong or God is failing; it is part of God's sovereign plan.
- *We have failed:* This is a reason to confess our sins, not to resist coming to God in prayer.
- *God keeps his promises anyway:* His promises can give us confidence, but we cannot presume on them.
- *Prayer never works:* Daniel 9:20-23 teaches us that the prayers of believers are heard in heaven, and answered (even though often we cannot see how they are being answered).
- *I don't know what to say:* Follow Daniel's example! Thank God for his character; confess your sin and the church's sins; ask God to have mercy on us for his sake, on the basis of his merciful character.

7

The Final Vision
Daniel 10 – 12

The Big Idea
We are heading toward the return of Jesus, when we will be bodily resurrected and live in glory with him; so we need to wait for that, keeping going in faith to the end.

Summary
In this last study, we look at Daniel's final vision, which lasts from 10:1 all the way through to the end of the book in 12:13.

The focus is on the elements and details that we have not already looked at as we have studied the first visions:

- the cost of receiving the vision.
- the lifting of the curtain to see the unseen universe, where each geopolitical kingdom has been assigned an angel (who are not all working in obedience to God and the good of his people)—see Explore More.
- more detail on what God's people will

face in the reign of Antiochus Epiphanes (and, because in apocalyptic literature symbols stand both for specific people or events, and for more general realities, what God's people will face in the time between the exile and the end, when Jesus returns).

- how God's people will be tempted to bring God's promises to fruition by their own efforts; fall away from faith; listen to the lies of God's enemies.
- the glorious future awaiting those who keep going to the end—bodily resurrection and eternity in glory with God.

Daniel is told to "roll up and seal" the vision (12:4)—it is not to be made known during his lifetime, perhaps because its fulfillment will not come for centuries. But we have the privilege of living after the death and resurrection of the Lord Jesus, and so we can understand more fully what Daniel saw—the gospel message is what makes clearer the truths of this vision (see 1 Peter 1:10-12).

So the aim of the study, like the aim of this vision (Daniel 12:12-13), is to encourage us to persevere to the end—to keep going in faith, even in the hardest of trials, waiting for the Lord Jesus to return, and bring resurrection and our inheritance.

Optional Extra

Prepare two trays, each containing 20 different objects. Ask two or three members of your group to look at the objects on the first tray for a minute, while everyone else is silent, and then write down what they saw on the tray.

Then repeat the exercise with the second tray, but this time, the rest of the group are allowed to distract them in any way they wish (other than physically!). It is a test of how easily distracted the people are as they seek to remember the objects; and an illustration of how easy it is for God's people to be tempted to cease waiting for the end, and be distracted by the powers and promises of this world.

Guidance for Questions

1. **What events or possibilities in your future most affect your actions and feelings in the present?**

   Encourage your group to think of things in this life (rather than death, and heaven beyond it). Examples could include retirement; the weekend; a holiday; children going to college; a promotion. Refer back to this question with reference to what God revealed of the future to Daniel (and to us) after question 9.

2. **Why is Daniel the only person to see the vision (v 4-9)?**

   Although unseen by everyone who was near Daniel at the time, the arrival of the man—the angel—seems to have overwhelmed them, and so "they fled and hid themselves" (v 7). Daniel was "left alone" (v 8).

- **How does he feel about seeing the "man dressed in linen" (v 8, 11, 16-17)?**
  - v 8: He had no strength left, went pale, and was "helpless."

- v 11: He was trembling.
- v 16-17: He was "overcome with anguish" and felt "very weak"—he could "hardly breathe."

3. **What are we seeing about the costs of being a prophet? How different is this from what you tend to think being a prophet would have been like?**

The prophetic office is not for everyone; and for those to whom it came, it did so with a cost—Daniel was exhausted, physically and emotionally, by the experience of seeing and receiving God's word. We tend to think that being a prophet—having revelation from God and being greatly used by God—was a great job: easy, respected, and bringing intimacy with God. Not so! It was an almost unbearable experience (see also Isaiah 6:1-5; Revelation 1:12-17a).

Explore More

○ *Reread Daniel 10:12-14; 10:20 – 11:1. Why did the angel not join Daniel earlier?*

Because he had had to struggle for 21 days in order to get past the "prince of the Persian kingdom," and had only done so because of assistance given by one of God's own "chief princes," Michael (10:13). Michael is also "your prince" (10:21)—Revelation 12:7 indicates that Michael is the "prince," or angel, who looks after Israel, the people of God.

○ *How does this glimpse of the unseen universe humble us as 21st-century humans?*

There is so much we do not know— and cannot ever come to know by observation of the seen universe. And there are great powers in play that we cannot understand or see.

4. **What effect will his reign have on God's people (v 28, 30-32)?**
   - v 28: He will "take action" against "the holy covenant"—that is, he will actively oppose those who are part of God's covenant people.
   - v 30-32: Again we are told he will war against the holy covenant (v 30). As a result of this opposition, some of God's people will forsake the holy covenant themselves (v 30). Further, servants of this ungodly ruler will appear and desecrate the temple and put an end to the regular burnt offering (v 31). And then, to add insult to injury, he will set up an idol in the holy place—an "abomination that causes desolation" (v 31). God's place will not be the only thing tarnished; the people will be as well. The evil king will seduce with flattery some of God's people—those who violate the covenant (v 32).

- **What mistakes will God's people make, or be tempted to make (v 14, 30, 32)?**
   - v 14: The king of the South likely refers to the king of Egypt (south of Israel). When many other nations

rise up against him, the struggling Jews will become involved, hoping that they might bring about the "fulfillment of the vision." Some will therefore be tempted to take matters into their own hands for their deliverance, rather than trusting in God to deliver them and fulfill his promises.

- v 30: "Forsake the holy covenant"— when persecution comes, so will the temptation to turn away from being part of God's people and from relying on God's promises.
- v 32: Some will be corrupted by flattery into serving an enemy of God's people, who opposes God.

- **What will "the wise" do (v 32-35)?**
  - They will resist the enemy of God, because they know God (v 32).
  - They will instruct many, even in hard times (that the kingdom of God comes through suffering) (v 33).
  - As they struggle through an age when culture promotes sinful rebellion, they will be "refined, purified and made spotless" (v 35). When the wise fail, they turn back to God, and it is used for their good.

5. **What would it look like for us as God's people to make the mistakes of verses 14, 30, and 32?**
Discuss how those three mistakes would look in your own particular culture (both around and within your church). There will be more than one right answer. Encourage your group to discuss their own temptations and struggles, rather than those of others.

- **How ought we to apply verses 32-35 to ourselves? (Read Mark 13:5-13, 32-37 for Jesus' help in answering this!)**
Jesus tells us what life will be like— as revealed to Daniel, it will be full of suffering and danger, even from those from whom we should expect to receive support and security (the courts, the family). And he tells us to stand firm to the end so that we might be saved; we are to be on guard and to keep watch, ready for his return, by continuing in faithful obedience.

6. **What will happen when deliverance finally arrives (v 2-3)?**
The multitudes of people who have died will "awake." Here, we find the clearest expression in all of the Old Testament of a literal, bodily resurrection from the dead. And notice that this is a double resurrection—that is, all of humanity is included, not merely the faithful. All will be raised, and some will enjoy "everlasting life," while others will endure "shame and everlasting contempt." If you have time, turn to Jesus' words about this event in Matthew 25:31-46.

NOTE: There are other passages in the Old Testament that suggest a bodily resurrection (e.g. Isaiah 26:19; Ezekiel 37; Psalm 16:9-10; Hosea 6:2). But no text in the entirety of the Old Testament reveals the promise of a bodily resurrection quite like Daniel 12:1-3.

7. **What must Daniel do, and until when (v 4)?**

"Roll up and seal the words of the scroll until the time of the end."

○ *OPTIONAL: Why is this a strange command?!*

Verses 1-3 promise God's people deliverance, bodily resurrection, and glorious eternal life—and Daniel was to write the vision down and then, strangely, put it on the shelf rather than make it known. We are right to ask why! Why would God want these words shut up and sealed?

• **Read 1 Peter 1:10-12. In what sense do we live in "the time of the end"? (See the words of the angel to Daniel in 12:4.)**

We live in the time when God's mysterious plan for the ages has been made known. Knowledge has increased (Daniel 12:4), and we now know in the gospel what the prophets, including Daniel, saw more dimly. We live in the time when what Daniel was to seal up—because it related to a time when deliverance had arrived and God's salvation had become clear—has been opened for all to know and understand. We should sense the privilege of living on this side of the resurrection of Jesus Christ.

○ *OPTIONAL [if you asked the previous extra question]: So why was Daniel told to seal the vision?*

Because its full understanding was not for Daniel, or those in his time,

but for those who would come later, in our time—when the salvation to which the vision pointed had come to fulfillment in Christ.

8. **What question is asked in verse 6?**

How long—how long will it be before the difficult days are past, and the amazing events of verses 2-3 arrive?

• **What answer is given, and how does Daniel feel about that answer (v 7-8)?**

The time before those events will last for "a time, times and half a time." Everything will be completed "when the power of the holy people has been finally broken" (v 7).

Daniel does not understand—unsurprisingly, since the answer is enigmatic to say the least! (And notice that when Daniel makes another attempt to put the question differently (v 8), he is politely told to go away (v 9)!)

NOTE: There is a note in the Study Guide (p. 51) suggesting how we might best understand the angel's answer, now that we have the advantage of Jesus' life, death, and resurrection being in the past, and not (as for Daniel) in the future.

9. **How should Daniel (and we) respond to this glimpse of the future (v 12-13)?**

He should hold on in faith (v 12), because the way to blessing—to enjoying life as it was designed to be, flourishing under God's good rule—is through waiting for, and reaching "the end" of this time, and seeing and welcoming God's deliverance when it comes. Daniel needs to carry on, to keep struggling on in faith, "till the end," when he will "rise" (v 13). So must we!

10. **How would the truths about God, the world, and the future that were revealed in these visions have enabled him to live as he did in Babylon, do you think?**

Remember that while the events of chapters 1 – 6 are in chronological, narrative order, the visions of chapters 7 – 12 do not follow on chronologically. Rather, they take place during the reigns of Belshazzar and Darius/Cyrus. So Daniel was being given these glimpses of the unseen universe and of the future as he faced the blessings and tensions of living as a member of God's people in Babylon. Surely the reason why he was able to see through the trinkets Belshazzar offered him, to have the courage to tell that king the truth about his heart and his reign, and to face the lions' den without compromising his obedience to God, was because he knew that the God he worshiped is the Ancient of Days (7:9-10). He knew that life would be tough, but deliverance would come; he knew that God is in charge.

11. **How does verse 13 both encourage and challenge you as a believer today?**

While we all yearn to know "how long," there is a more important question: what am I doing to prepare? While we all want to rest from our labors, this passage tells us that for now, we need to labor on, in Christ, toward rest and resurrection. The angel's final words in verse 13 to Daniel must have encouraged him to do the same and, as we conclude these studies together in Daniel, my prayer is that it encourages us all to labor on, in Christ, toward glory, obeying him courageously in this world as we walk on home to our place with Christ.

12. **What difference has the book of Daniel made to...**
   • **your view of God?**
   • **your understanding of what it will mean for you to worship him?**
   • **your obedience in difficult circumstances?**

Give your group time to fill in each part on their own. Then, if time allows, share what you have each written, and use this to guide your prayers as you finish.

Go Deeper with the Expository Guide to

Daniel

by David Helm

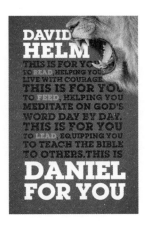

Less academic than a traditional commentary, this expository guide by David Helm takes you through the book of Daniel verse by verse. See how Daniel and his friends learned to live in Babylon, far from their home in God's land — and how we can do the same.

This flexible resource can enrich your personal devotions, help you lead small-group studies, or aid your sermon preparations.

Explore the God's Word For You series

thegoodbook.com/for-you
thegoodbook.co.uk/for-you
thegoodbook.com.au/for-you

Explore the Whole Range

Old Testament, including:

Tim Chester
Exodus
Liberating Love

Timothy Keller
Judges
The Flawed and the Flawless

Kathleen B. Nielson and Rachel Jones
Proverbs
Real Wisdom for Real Life

David Helm
Daniel
Staying Strong in a Hostile World

New Testament, including:

Josh Moody
John 1–12
Life to the Full

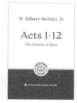
R. Albert Mohler Jr
Acts 1-12
The Church is Born

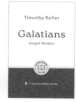
Timothy Keller
Galatians
Gospel Matters

Michael Kruger
Hebrews
An Anchor for the Soul

Topical, including:

Carl Laferton
Promises Kept
The Whole Story of the Bible

Anne Woodcock
Joy
Happiness of the Heart

Jason Helopoulos
The Five Solas
Three Truths Alone

Tim Chester
The Lord's Prayer
Talking to Our Father

Flexible and easy to use, with over 50 titles available,
Good Book Guides are perfect for both groups and individuals.

thegoodbook.com/gbgs
thegoodbook.co.uk/gbgs
thegoodbook.com.au/gbgs

GOOD BOOK GUIDE

thegoodbook

COMPANY

BIBLICAL | RELEVANT | ACCESSIBLE

At The Good Book Company we are dedicated to helping Christians and local churches grow. We believe that God's growth process always starts with hearing clearly what he has said to us through his timeless and flawless word—the Bible.

Ever since we opened our doors in 1991, we have been striving to produce resources that are biblical, relevant, and accessible. By God's grace, we have grown to become an international publisher, encouraging ordinary Christians of every age and stage and every background and denomination to live for Christ day by day and equipping churches to grow in their knowledge of God, their love for one another, and the effectiveness of their outreach.

Call one of our friendly team for a discussion of your needs or visit one of our local websites for more information on the resources and services we provide.

Your friends at The Good Book Company

thegoodbook.com | thegoodbook.co.uk
thegoodbook.com.au | thegoodbook.co.nz
thegoodbook.co.in